QUEBEC

DURING THE
AMERICAN INVASION,
1775–1776

Quebec

during the American Invasion, 1775–1776

THE JOURNAL *of* FRANÇOIS BABY,
GABRIEL TASCHEREAU, *and* JENKIN WILLIAMS

Michael P. Gabriel, *Editor*
S. Pascale Vergereau-Dewey, *Translator*

Michigan State University Press • *East Lansing*

♾ The paper used in this publication meets the minimum requirements
of ANSI/NISO Z39.48-1992 (R 1997) (Permanence of Paper).

Michigan State University Press
East Lansing, Michigan 48823-5245

Printed and bound in the United States of America.

11 10 09 08 07 06 05   1 2 3 4 5 6 7 8 9 10

LIBRARY OF CONGRESS CATALOGING-IN-PUBLICATION DATA
Baby, François, 1733–1820.
[Journal de MM. Baby, Taschereau et Williams, 1776. English]
Québec during the American invasion, 1775–1776 : the journal of François Baby, Gabriel Taschereau,
and Jenkin Williams / Michael P. Gabriel, editor; S. Pascale Vergereau-Dewey, translator.
p. cm.
Includes bibliographical references and index.
ISBN 0-87013-740-9 (pbk. : alk. paper)
1. Canadian Invasion, 1775–1776—Personal narratives. 2. United States—History—Revolution,
1775–1783—Collaborationists. 3. Collaborationists—Québec (Province)—History—18th century.
4. Québec (Province)—Description and travel. 5. Trois-Rivières (Québec)—Description and travel.
6. Baby, François, 1733–1820—Diaries. 7. Taschereau, Gabriel-Elzéar, 1745–1809—Diaries.
8. Williams, Jenkin, d. 1819—Diaries. 9. Canada—Officials and employees—Diaries. 10. United States—
History—Revolution, 1775–1783—Personal narratives. I. Taschereau, Gabriel-Elzéar, 1745–1809.
II. Williams, Jenkin, d. 1819. III. Gabriel, Michael P., 1962– IV. Title.
E231.B125 2005
971.4'45102—dc22
2004025631

Cover design by Erin Kirk New.
Book design by Sharp Des!gns, Inc., Lansing, MI.
Cover art: L'Honorable François Baby, by Lt. Col. A.-D. Aubry.
Courtesy of the National Archives of Canada (C 8852).

Michigan State University Press is a member of the Green Press Initiative and is committed to developing
and encouraging ecologically responsible publishing practices. For more information about the Green Press
Initiative and the use of recycled paper in book publishing, please visit www.greenpressinitiative.com

Visit Michigan State University Press on the World Wide Web at www.msupress.msu.edu

Contents

BABY JOURNAL

Maps and Illustrations

for the Baby Journal

Acknowledgments

WE WOULD LIKE TO THANK THE MANY PEOPLE AND ORGANIZATIONS THAT helped us complete this project. The New-York Historical Society, Independence National Historical Park, Library of Congress, New York Public Library, and National Archives of Canada provided us with illustrations for the book. Our thanks also go to Associated University Presses, which allowed us to reprint parts of a previous work in the introduction. Martha Bates and Julie L. Loehr at Michigan State University Press guided us through the publication process. Most important, we wish to thank Karen Krugh, chair of the Kutztown University Research Committee, and its members for their efforts on our behalf in securing a grant that made the completion of this book possible.

S. Pascale Vergereau-Dewey additionally wishes to acknowledge with thanks Bruce Ezell, former dean of Graduate Studies at Kutztown University, and Dale Titus, who introduced her to Drs. Robert Timko and Larry Biddison, devoted Canadianists and respectively past and present directors of the Pennsylvania Consortium for Canadian Studies at Mansfield University of Pennsylvania. Both have become appreciated colleagues who made it possible for me to be awarded grants to visit Canada. This opened an exciting new field of study on the history of New France and the French presence on the North American continent, both in Canada and in the United States. It also gave me the opportunity to meet and befriend Professor Emeritus Dr. Louis Balthazar, the former chair of the Department of Political Science at University Laval, who most readily and graciously contributed an introduction to our book.

The original idea for this book, however, came from Mike Gabriel. I would like to thank him for his patience and assistance as my co-editor. I would be remiss not to mention the help of Laurence Porter from the University of Michigan in locating Joseph I. Donohoe Jr., who graciously accepted to be a final reviewer for our manuscript. His sharp eye eliminated errors and inconsistencies. To all I am most grateful.

Michael P. Gabriel would like to thank William A. Pencak of Penn State University. Bill immediately recognized the value of the Baby manuscript and was the first to encourage me to publish it. Jean-Yves Rousseau, Denis Plante, and Michel Champagne of the Archives Division at the University of Montreal granted us permission to translate and edit the Baby journal. They also provided a photocopy and photograph of the original manuscript. Panelists, commentators, and members of the audience at several conferences helped me formulate my ideas as I presented parts of my research as papers. My friends and colleagues in the Department of History at Kutztown University also deserve my thanks. Michael D. Gambone strengthened an early draft of the introduction with valuable insights. Graduate assistants Tom Beil, Melinda Scheel, Karen Breidinger-Trinkle, and Vaneesa Cook ran down numerous small details and helped identify many of the individuals mentioned in the manuscript. Department of History secretary Judy Groff provided invaluable assistance in preparing the final version of the text and is always a good friend.

Several others deserve special recognition. Pascale Vergereau-Dewey did a wonderful job of translating the manuscript, and I thank her for all her work and suggestions. I also want to thank my family for encouraging my love of history. Finally and most important, I want to thank my new bride, Sandy, for her unwavering faith in me and in this project. Sandy read numerous drafts, helped me select illustrations for the book, and always believed in my work. I dedicate this book to her.

Foreword

THE FOLLOWING DOCUMENT, ALTHOUGH PUBLISHED IN FRENCH IN 1928, IS A revelation for most people in Quebec as well as for English-speaking readers. I confess my own astonishment. I never thought that the 1775 population of the old Province of Quebec, as Canada was then called (mainly those who were called "*habitants*," that is to say, the farm population) had expressed so much support for the American Revolution.

Quite paradoxically, Great Britain was more successful in protecting Canada, a colony peopled with its former French enemies, than in keeping its own colonies settled by a population mostly of British extraction. While a revolutionary spirit animated the thirteen American colonies from the early 1770s on, Canada seemed to remain quiet and prepared to ensure a safe haven to loyalists or Tories. One may wonder why a French population that had just been conquered in 1760 would not be tempted to escape British domination by joining the American Revolution. This would make even more sense when France, the old home country for most Canadians, would bring its support to the American military uprising.[1] But France, for a number of reasons related to its European concerns, did not seek to regain control of Canada.

The American revolutionaries did their best to conclude an alliance with the Canadians in order to drive Great Britain from the continent completely. On October 26, 1774, representatives at the Philadelphia Congress sent an address to their northern neighbors inviting them to make common cause with them. It was written in French by Fleury de Mesplet, a printer working for Congress, and entitled "*L'appel du Congrès aux Canadiens*" (A call from Congress to Canadians). The object of the message was to deliver Canadians from oppression, despotism, and tyranny. The people's inalienable rights were enumerated, such as a house of assembly, habeas corpus, freedom of expression and religion, and the power to make laws. Canadians were enjoined to refrain from opposing the American military and invited to unite with Americans by "a social pact, founded on the principle of equal liberty."[2]

In fact, this invitation did not fall on deaf ears. When American troops did invade Canada in the summer of 1775, the British colonial government tried to enroll *habitants* and met with resistance, "which amounted almost to rebellion against the state."[3] As this publication will document abundantly, the great majority of Canadians either supported the invasion or remained neutral. Nonetheless, after occupying Montreal, American troops, led by Richard Montgomery and Benedict Arnold, failed to take the fortress of Quebec.

Later on, in the spring of 1776, the Continental Congress sent Benjamin Franklin to Montreal, conveniently accompanied by Roman Catholic bishop John Carroll and Fleury de Mesplet, to induce the Canadians into joining the American cause. The delegation was unsuccessful. The leaders of the Canadian community, landlords and religious authorities, resisted their appeal. Canadians remained loyal to the crown.

Why? The main reason seems to reside in a very clever move on the part of the British government. At the call of the governor of the colony, Guy Carleton, the Quebec Act was passed by Westminster and sanctioned by the king. The act recognized, for the most part, the existence of a specific culture in the Province of Quebec. It authorized the old French system of civil law, inspired by the "Paris Custom," including a tenure regime that was a lenient form of feudalism. It also exempted, for the first time in the British Empire, the Canadian population from the Test Oath, which required any civil servant to abjure parts of the Roman Catholic doctrine. It enlarged the territory of Canada to include Indian territories of the Midwest, which particularly infuriated the American Congress. This act, cited in the Declaration of Independence as one of the 1774 Intolerable Acts, had much to please Canadians who had become attached to their old laws, to their seigniorial regime, and, above all, to their Catholic religion. Although the act did not mention the French language specifically, it ensured a certain protection of it, since the old laws were all written in French, while religious sermons and catechism were delivered mainly in that language. Canadian leaders especially were quite pleased with the act. Landlords, the seigneurs, saw their authority confirmed, and the Catholic hierarchy was happy to see its religion recognized. It was the beginning of a long informal alliance between British authorities and the Canadian bishops. As a consequence, when Franklin called for Canadian support, the people he talked to could respond that they much preferred the certainty of recognition by the crown to the uncertain future of an American republic.

Moreover, Canadians were naturally somewhat reluctant to embrace the cause of their former enemies. For more than a century before 1760, they had grown accustomed to be at war periodically with the people they called the "*Bostonnais*." They may have resented British dominance, but they were equally suspicious of British colonists, with whom they had little in common. In fact, Canadians had not been much aware of the doctrine of Enlightenment and were still imbued with an old regime mentality. There was no press and no popular representative assembly in the French colonial system.

There was nonetheless a little commercial bourgeoisie in Canada. But it was mostly decimated by the British conquest so that in the crucial years of 1775–76, a committed leadership did not organize the cause of support to the American Revolution. There were no enlightened leaders in the Province of Quebec. Therefore, as broad and strong as sympathy could be for American rebels, it remained spasmodic, erratic, and mostly passive. As one Canadian historian put it, a farm population like the Canadians, recently conquered and deprived of any military organization other than the British, could make only two important contributions: "supplying of the armed forces with food and providing a friendly countryside through which armies had to march and both contributions were made by the Canadian farm population."[4]

This is what the following pages will show with striking evidence. British authorities had good reasons not to publicize what they had found through a commission of inquiry in many Canadian parishes. As a consequence, the following document remained for a long time widely unknown, and it was believed that the Canadian population had stood quite loyal to its colonial government during the American revolutionaries' invasion. Fortunately, however, a copy of the major part of the report to the British governor was saved and made public by the archivist of the Province of Quebec. It may not provide for easy reading in its very technocratic form, but it is a fascinating testimony of widespread support for the American revolutionaries among the Canadian *habitants*. This was especially true in the region around Quebec City, where the last unsuccessful offensive was carried out. A great number of *habitants*, many of whom had been commissioned by the government to fight against the invaders, rallied to the rebels' cause. It is not rare to find in the report sentences like, "Almost everyone from this parish seems to have aided and assisted the rebels with much zeal." Indeed, the reader cannot but infer from this report that, had there been an organized and democratic referendum in the province, support for the American Revolution would have won handily at that time.

How come, then, this support did not materialize in the following years? Was this revolutionary sympathy completely smothered? Not quite. Fleury de Mesplet, the printer who had sent the Continental Congress's address to Canadians in 1774 and had come along with Franklin in 1776, stayed in Montreal for the rest of his life. He founded a newspaper, the *Montreal Gazette*, first published in French, which spread enlightened ideas. Several Canadians joined those British and loyalist citizens who called for a representative assembly. This assembly did materialize in the Constitutional Act of 1791, but it was less than a half victory for democracy since the assembly had no real control over the treasury. It became the center of ethnic conflict between the French-speaking Canadians, who soon dominated the assembly, and the British and loyalist minority. This conflict diluted the real opposition to British autocracy. The government, for its part, nurtured a system of patronage that could partially stifle and assuage opposition. But when Canadians were called to fight their republican neighbors in 1814, they responded in a lukewarm way.

By the 1830s, the colonial system had come to a stalemate between the British government and an aggressive assembly in which some English-speaking members had joined the opposition of the Canadian majority. It led to a violent rebellion, which was finally crushed thanks to the loyalty of the Roman Catholic hierarchy and some Canadian elite. The rebels' leader, Louis Joseph Papineau, fled to the United States in exile and sought support from the American government, without any concrete results. Americans had developed a foreign policy that was far from being antagonistic to the former metropolis. They would not jeopardize smooth relations with Great Britain for the sake of an unknown population to the North.

Thus there was never a revolution in Canada. Canadians finally obtained democracy but in a slow and evolutionary way. Only when the English-speaking population became the majority did it claim the title of Canadian and was a form of government control conferred upon the legislature. French Canadians became a minority and were considered for almost a century as the backward element in the country. Their elite remained quite conservative, but it would be a mistake to conclude that any enlightened spirit had deserted them. This spirit came alive with the so-called quiet revolution of the 1960s.

What is striking throughout this historical evolution to this day is the profound ambivalence of the Quebec people toward the system that ruled them. They more or less accepted British dominance because they were recognized in their distinctive character by the Quebec Act. They subscribed to confederation in 1867 because they obtained a provincial government in which they were the majority, with some important powers in vital sectors. They would gladly embrace federalism today as long as its main principles are respected and they are allowed to maintain a strong collective identity in the province of Quebec. They appreciate their Canadian identity, but they strongly resent a "national" government that would slowly erode the power of their own Quebec government. In great number, they feel threatened by a Canadian nationalist movement that does not leave much room for their basic Quebec identity.

A similar form of ambivalence affected those *habitants* who welcomed the American rebels but could not finally get organized to join the American

Revolution. Again today, more than two hundred years later, Quebeckers are quite fascinated with Americans. They have given their strong and whole-hearted support to a free trade agreement with the United States. They travel in great numbers to the neighboring country. They love American culture, but they take a different stand. They stick to the French language. They watch their own television shows and enjoy their own cultural productions. They are even exporting them. For a small population of some seven million, it is at the same time quite a feat and quite a challenge.

As much as it was in 1775, they feel part of America and what it represents, but they are not willing to be engulfed by the United States. They are often in conflict with their federal government and frequently seem more attracted by their southern neighbors than by the East-West system. But for the time being, they want to remain a part of Canada. The reader will find in the following pages a confirmation that this ambivalence is profoundly rooted in history.

Louis Balthazar

Professor emeritus, Department of Political Science, University Laval

Preface
to the Current Edition

IN 1791, THOMAS JEFFERSON ESTABLISHED A RATIONALE FOR EDITING HISTORIC documents that still rings true:

> Time and accident are committing daily havoc on the originals [documents] deposited in our public offices. . . . The lost cannot be recovered; but let us save what remains: not by vaults and locks which fence them from the public eye and use, in consigning them to the waste of time, but by such a multiplication of copies, as shall place them beyond the reach of accident.[1]

One such document that should be saved from "the waste of time" is the 1776 journal of François Baby, Gabriel-Elzéar Taschereau, and Jenkin Williams, hereafter referred to as the Baby journal. Canadian governor Sir Guy Carleton commissioned this report by three trusted envoys to discover who collaborated with the Americans during their 1775–76 invasion of the province.[2] The three commissioners traveled to fifty-six parishes and missions in the Quebec and Trois Rivières districts, discharging disloyal militia officers and replacing them with faithful subjects.[3] They also wrote a report on each parish, revealing who had done what to support the Americans or the king.

The Baby journal provides fascinating insights into Quebec during the American Revolution at the local level. While other sources have shown how British soldiers and civilians and the French Canadian gentry, the seigneurs, responded to the Americans, the Baby journal is unique.[4] Unlike any other

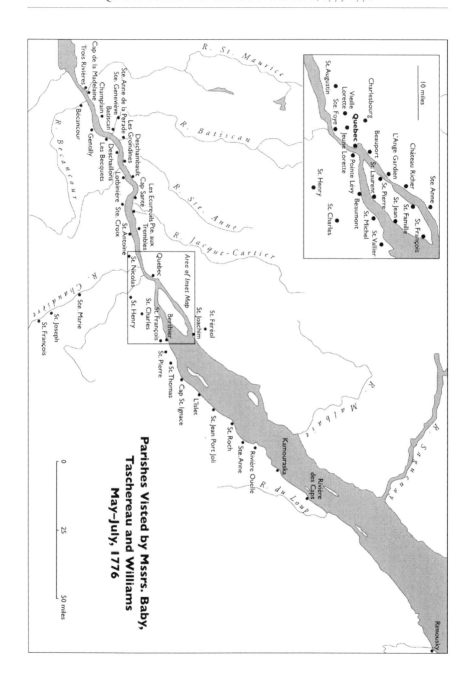

Parishes Visited by Mssrs. Baby, Taschereau and Williams
May–July, 1776

document, it focuses on the French Canadian peasants, *les habitants*, who made up the vast majority of the population. Furthermore, the Baby journal greatly adds to our knowledge of the American Revolution and helps explain why Quebec did not become the "fourteenth colony."

This is not the first version of the Baby journal to appear in print. Aegidius Fauteux edited a version in French for the *Rapport de L'Archiviste de la Province de Québec* in 1927–28 and 1929–30, and the journal was released as a separate monograph in 1929.[5] Since then, such Canadian historians as Gustave Lanctôt have cited it extensively.[6] Still, the journal has never appeared in English and remains largely unfamiliar to historians who do not read French. This should be rectified.

About the Translation

The Baby journal is quite typical of eighteenth-century writings by military and diplomatic emissaries on an official mission in its format and administrative style. Yet it is also unique in its content. It sheds light on the state of local affairs in Quebec during the American Revolution. The copyist who wrote the manuscript in 1776 had beautiful penmanship, which eliminated one of the principal problems of translating and transcribing such a document. Still, one had to remain alert for the Baby copyist's own stylistic idiosyncrasies. The manuscript contains frequent grammatical lapses, such as incorrect agreement of subject and verb, incorrect sequences of tense, and omissions of words that had to be inferred from the meaning of the sentence. The Baby journal also contains a large number of misspelled words, especially of place names, such as *lisle d'Orlean*. Furthermore, many of the sentences are extremely long, and some passages are not even sentences at all. This is partly caused by erratic punctuation. The use of accent marks is similarly irregular at best.

Another challenge in translating the Baby journal is the terminology that the copyist employed. The manuscript contains archaisms, such as *les sieurs* and *bonhomme*, which have been left to give the reader a feel for the original usage. The document is also inconsistent in its spellings of locations and abbreviations of names. The use of contemporary maps and gazetteers helped

General Sir Guy Carleton, by Mabel B. Messer. Courtesy of the National Archives of Canada (C-2833).

identify some of the former cases. A translator also needed to be familiar with eighteenth-century military, commercial, religious, and other terms, such as *fascines*. These long bundles of sticks were used like sandbags in siege warfare; the word also means fishing nets. Finally, the Baby journal is interesting in its use of both Anglicisms, such as *deux shelins par jour*, and Quebeckisms, such as *les habitants*. This reflects the mixing of cultures following the British conquest in 1763. The journal also provides numerous examples of the common French Canadian practice of men using "aliases" rather than their given names, such as Laurent Genais *dit* Labarre.

In translating the Baby journal, the translator's goal was to render an accurate and legible English equivalent of the manuscript without losing the flavor of its original context. Reconciling the dynamics of the original text with an idiomatic translation that expresses the source's intended meaning in a natural form is a delicate balancing act. Therefore, whenever possible, the translator reduced lengthy passages to more manageable sentence fragments, adding punctuation and making minor but necessary changes in wording. At the same time, she retained the author's choice of key words and phrases to give the reader some of the flavor and structure of the original document. However, she sought to avoid translating too literally, which would have resulted in unnatural or stilted wording. Generally, the translator corrected the Baby journal's irregular syntax and spelling but always strove to convey the precise thoughts of the author. She similarly tried to do this in a number of dialogues, which were curiously transcribed in direct style when the indirect style would have been more appropriate. Abbreviations in the manuscript itself follow French usage. If the abbreviation ends in the same letter as the unabbreviated word, no period is placed at the end of it. A list of abbreviations that appear in the Baby journal has been included to assist the reader.

The translated Baby journal contains two passages that were either crossed out or erased in the original but were still visible. These are indicated with struck-through characters in the text. Similarly, words or phrases missing from the Fauteux version but contained in the handwritten one are underlined in the text. When an individual's name was spelled differently in two places, the first spelling was placed in brackets after the alternative.

In addition to a map and illustrations, this version of the Baby journal includes several features to assist readers. Particular events and individuals have been annotated to provide a greater understanding of the journal and its times. This edition also contains an itinerary that lists each parish and the date that the commissioners visited it. The itinerary also contains the page number of the parish reports in both the original 1776 manuscript and the 1927 Fauteux edition.

Preface
to the 1927 Edition

A 1775–1776 Journal

The following published journal is an historical document of the utmost significance. It consists of a minutely detailed report by three special envoys, Messrs. Baby, Taschereau and Williams specially commissioned by Governor Carleton to make an inquiry while touring various parishes of the Quebec district in 1776.

According to the document title, these commissaries had received a two-fold mission that of establishing a militia in each parish and that of cross-examining people who had assisted rebels during the American invasion the previous year. In reality, this dual mission had a single objective, which was to re-organize the militia, since pre-existing troops had disbanded or had been neutralized due to the population's sympathy towards congregationists [Americans] or simply as a result of the people's indifference. The true object of the mission was to estimate the degree of loyalty in the various parishes of the Quebec District, to punish the traitors and acknowledge the loyalty of the others. We will be given ample opportunities to measure the zeal of Carleton's emissaries and appreciate to what extent they fulfilled their charge; the detail of their extraordinary perquisitions is, indeed, as intriguing as it is informative.

Aegidus Fauteux, "Journal par Messrs Frans Baby, Gab. Taschereau et Jenkin Williams dans la Tournée qu'ils ont fait dans le District de Québec. . . ." *Rapport de L'Archiviste de la Province de Québec* (1927–1928): 431–34.

This document is a new source of information, which adds to the others and to all that we already know about the 1775 invasion. Historians, undoubtedly, will welcome it as one of the most precious sources of reference when studying a very critical moment of our national past. Many memoirs and newspapers have been unearthed in the course of these past years. To be sure, all prove to be of great help in understanding the military aspect of Montgomery and Arnold's undertaking; however, none of them to date, not even Lorimier's, Sanguinet's or Badeaux's allow us to understand the given situation in such detail as the Baby, Taschereau and Williams account. Their report seems to reflect those troubled times with an incredible clarity that mirrors the feelings and the mood of the population of Lower Canada in 1775.

Curiously we have been unable to find any trace in our Archives of this mission which Messrs. Baby, Taschereau and Williams were asked to undertake. Carleton himself does not mention it in his correspondence to Germaine when he touches upon the topic of Canadians' loyalism in several of his letters. The governor, most likely, looked upon the inquiry he had ordered as nothing more than a routine measure concerning internal affairs. Perhaps he deemed it sufficient to draw from it some general conclusions that he passed on to London for information purposes. After researching all the available historical data relating to this period, we came across only two vague mentions which seem to refer to the Baby-Taschereau-Williams mission: these allusions appear in the body of two letters François Baby himself received from his sister, the widow Benoît, letters which Vicar Verreau published in his work *Invasion du Canada (The Invasion of Canada)*. A first time, on August 12, 1776, Mrs. Benoît writes to her beloved brother that she is very flattered to see him in charge of one of the Province's most sensitive and delicate missions, an honor which points to the degree of confidence his Excellency, the General, puts in Baby's talents. A bit later, on December 11, Mrs. Benoît complains that she does not hear from her brother very often. She thinks, however, that only his many responsibilities have kept M. Baby from writing to her adding: "I think that it is a formidable task to bring back rebels into the fold and remind them of their dutiful allegiance." We confess that without the discovery of the report we are publishing today, these few lines by Mrs. Benoît would remain forever puzzling. One must not be surprised, therefore, to find out that no historian to this day has ever commented on them.

When Smith, Bibaud, Garneau or even M. Chapais tried to render the mood that prevailed amidst the general population in 1775, none of them seem to have consulted Baby's report or if they did, they did not mention it. The obvious reason would be that they were not even aware of its existence. As far as we know, the most learned and maybe the wisest amongst all researchers, M. J. Edmond Roy, was the first to make use of this precious piece of evidence for a book he was to publish. He was the first to even mention its existence. He directly quoted some remarkable excerpts in the index of his third and fourth volumes of *Histoire de la Seigneurerie de Lauzon* (*History of the Lauzon Seignieury*). Following his lead, in 1917, M. L'abbé Auguste Gosselin in the second part of his *Eglise du Canada depuis la conquête,* (*The Church in Canada since the Conquest*) attempted to summarize the same document in a more succinct manner.

Neither M. Roy's excerpts nor M. Gosselin's summary adequately reflect the Baby, Taschereau and Williams report. All who purport to study Canadian history will appreciate the decision of the Quebec Office of Archives to disclose and make public this original text in its entirety.

This journal is hereby reproduced from a manuscript the Honorable F. G. Baby donated to Montreal University. It is deposited at the Saint-Sulpice Library of Montreal along with the learned antique dealer's precious Canadian collection. The manuscript consists of 172 pages petit in-quarto. It is handwritten in 1776 style. Nothing allows us to conclude that it was written by one of the three envoys. It seems to be the work of a scribe or a secretary. Since it was found in the Baby Collection, we could infer that the copy we used is the very copy that belonged to François Baby. Does that mean then that there might have been a single copy the senior investigator reserved for his own use, a copy that his family might have kept? This question must remain unanswered. Maybe somewhere another copy of this official document is to be found in the Dorchester family's archives. We can only hope that if indeed, such a document does exist, it will be discovered some day to confirm that ours, unfortunately, is incomplete. Not only have two pages been torn out by an unknown vandal but the entire ending of the manuscript is missing. We have only the report of the last sessions of the inquiry after July 14, 1776. This account tells us that the report published herein was continued in a small notebook, which has not yet been found.

Be that as it may, and in the condition now presented to the public, the Baby's report—as it has come to be known, named after the older of the three emissaries—will doubtless be recognized as a contribution of the utmost significance.

Aegidius Fauteux

Introduction

TO FULLY APPRECIATE THE BABY JOURNAL, IT IS USEFUL TO KNOW THE CON-text in which it was written and understand some of the events that it chron-icles. At the end of the Seven Years' War in 1763, the Treaty of Paris transferred ownership of Canada to Britain from France. Britain, however, had a difficult task in making loyal, contented subjects of the sixty thousand to seventy thousand Catholic French Canadians who lived there. The British brought greater economic stability, which allowed the French Canadians to grow more prosperous and accepting of their rule. The *habitants* also gained because, under the British, the French Canadian gentry, the seigneurs, lost their feudal privileges over the peasantry.

Still, the governance system left much to be desired from the French Canadian perspective. In the years immediately after the treaty, Britain ruled Canada by a royal edict dated October 7, 1763, which created the province of Quebec. This enactment limited Quebec's geographic boundaries to a rectan-gle along the St. Lawrence Valley, rather than its original ones of the Missis-sippi River in the west, Hudson Bay to the north, and Labrador in the east. It also created a governor who would rule with the assistance of an appointed council. The edict called for the eventual creation of an elected assembly but did not set a timetable for it. Finally, the October ruling called for the cre-ation of courts based on English law. This system effectively banned the par-ticipation of Catholic French Canadians by requiring an oath acknowledging the Protestant succession in Britain.

Generals James Murray and Sir Guy Carleton, Quebec's first two governors, realized that this system was unacceptable to most Canadians and lobbied for the creation of a new government.[1] This was accomplished in June 1774, when Parliament passed the Quebec Act. The bill's main provisions recognized Catholicism in Canada, restored the province's original borders, enlarged Quebec's appointed council, and reestablished French civil law while retaining British criminal law. It also allowed Catholics to participate in governance by eliminating the Oath of Supremacy to the king.[2]

While the Canadians adjusted to British rule, the American colonists to the south increasingly came into conflict with the home country. Following the Seven Years' War, Britain enacted new policies to reduce its staggering national debt and administer its vastly enlarged empire. It closed the trans-Appalachian region to settlement and permanently deployed ten thousand British troops in North America. Parliament also increased enforcement of the Navigation Acts and passed unprecedented taxes, such as the Stamp Act of 1765 and the Townshend Duties of 1767, to finance American defense.

Britain's new policies raised a variety of constitutional and economic issues that centered on America's place in the empire and parliamentary supremacy. These new enactments could not have come at a worse time for the colonists, who were mired in an economic recession that struck at the close of the Seven Years' War. Many Americans began to blame the downturn on British actions. A widespread American fear of ministerial corruption and the concomitant belief in a conspiracy against liberty added to the tension. Each new parliamentary enactment further convinced Americans that a dissolute ministry aimed to deprive them of their rights as Englishmen.[3]

The drift toward conflict accelerated following Parliament's passage of the Coercive Acts in spring 1774 to punish Massachusetts for the Boston Tea Party. Among other things, the Intolerable Acts, as they were known to the Americans, closed the port of Boston and reduced self-government in Massachusetts. Although the Quebec Act was not part of the Coercive Acts, its passage in such close proximity to the others led Americans to consider it as one. In September and October 1774, the Americans met in Philadelphia for the First Continental Congress to develop a united response to Parliament's actions. While they condemned the Quebec Act for recognizing Catholicism and extending the province's borders to the Ohio River, the delegates also sent a letter to the Canadians requesting their support. Dated October 26, the letter claimed that the French Canadians faced despotism under the Quebec Act and invited them to send delegates to the congress that was scheduled to meet the following May.[4]

In spring 1775, after fighting broke out at Lexington and Concord in Massachusetts and the Second Continental Congress convened on May 10, the Americans continued to woo the Canadians. On May 29, 1775, Congress sent another letter to them. Addressed to "Friends and Countrymen," the letter explained the colonists' actions and warned the Canadians of the dangers that they, too, faced. "By the introduction of your present form of government, or rather present form of tyranny, you and your wives and your children are made slaves." It noted that "an avaritious governor and a rapacious council" could demand the "fruits of your labor and industry" whenever they desired. Canadians could also be forced to fight beyond their borders in a war that was not their own, and their religion "depends upon a legislature in which you have no share." The letter closed with an appeal for support: "We yet entertain hopes of your uniting with us in the defence of our common liberty." Congress ordered that a thousand copies of the letter be printed in French and sent to the province.[5]

Whether the Catholic French Canadians would support the Protestant Americans, their longtime enemies, was uncertain, but the Americans had some reason to be cautiously optimistic. Although the British had made a concerted effort to win over the French Canadians, the Quebec Act had not completely satisfied them. In this, they were partly influenced by the three hundred to two thousand English and American merchants and traders who had settled in Canada since 1763, especially near Montreal. Economic opportunity and the fur trade attracted many of these people. These so-called Old Subjects (subjects before the French Canadians) had a heritage of political rights not found among the French. The Old Subjects petitioned for the Quebec Act's repeal because it failed to provide for an elected assembly, although they had requested one for eleven years. They also disliked French civil law, believing it did not adequately protect trial by jury. Many of these merchants maintained contact with the American colonies. In March 1775, the Boston Committee of Correspondence sent an envoy to Montreal to apprise the Old Subjects of the situation in America and to judge their temperament. He found them sympathetic but not necessarily supportive, as they did not wish to jeopardize the fur trade.[6]

The Old Subjects' opposition to the Quebec Act influenced the *habitants*. The seigneurs and the clergy accepted British rule because the Quebec Act made them eligible to serve in the council and recognized Catholicism, but the *habitants'* support was much more problematic. In June 1775, one British loyalist, Thomas Ainslie, commented that "the Canadian Peasants began to shew a disposition little to be expected from a conquer'd people who had been treated with so much lenity by Government." The peasantry was partly influenced by "the never ceasing labours of the Malcontents in this Province," who clamored against the Quebec Act.[7] Furthermore, the French Canadians had not completely adjusted to British rule, having to overcome generations of hatred. They also possessed little respect for the seigneurs, who now heavily depended on the British for positions and status. The Quebec Act itself caused some resentment by allowing priests again to collect a tithe, which had been largely discontinued after 1763. Many *habitants* disliked British criminal law, and the act restored the seigneurs' feudal privileges over their tenants. The relative weakness of British forces in Canada also made the peasants hesitant to embrace England if a revolt occurred in America. Only two undersized regiments garrisoned the entire St. Lawrence Valley, as Carleton had dispatched two others to Boston, and a third was scattered throughout the Great Lakes region.[8]

In summer and fall 1775, Carleton compounded these bad feelings by having seigneurs recruit Canadians to defend the province and possibly serve against the Americans. The seigneurs' feudal presumptions and haughty attitude made the situation worse. They proclaimed that their tenants owed them military service and threatened to send British troops to pillage those who refused to comply. This was the very warning that Congress's letter had transmitted, and many *habitants* resisted. The most extreme case of this resistance occurred near Chambly on the Richelieu River, where the *habitants* thrashed their seigneur's son when he arrogantly ordered them to enlist. Three thousand Canadians then armed themselves and marched on the British garrison at St. Jeans. They finally dispersed after receiving word from Carleton that he would not move against them if they returned to their homes. Similar events took place in other areas near Montreal and, as the Baby journal makes apparent, they also occurred near Quebec.[9] At least nine parishes in the Quebec district refused to have officers appointed. The *habitants* at Pointe Lévy held a "seditious assembly" at which they invited neighboring parishes to resist British efforts. Furthermore, fourteen parishes posted guards to protect themselves from British troops or provided them for other towns.

While this unrest took place in Canada, Congress debated what to do about the northern province. Congress did not want to expand the war and possibly alienate the French Canadians, yet it received reports of British military preparations there. After changing its decisions a number of times, on June 27, 1775, Congress finally authorized American forces to "take possession of St. Johns, Montreal, and any other parts of the country, and pursue any other measures . . . , which may have a tendency to promote the peace and security of these Colonies." Congress prefaced its order with the phrase, if "it will not be disagreeable to the Canadians," demonstrating its awareness of the importance of the civilian population.[10] Congress not only hoped to remove permanently the British threat to the northern frontier and demonstrate American resolve to the ministry but also expand the rebellion's base of support.

In late August 1775, Brigadier General Richard Montgomery led American troops down Lake Champlain into Canada. By mid-November, Montgomery's army had captured Forts St. Jeans and Chambly on the Richelieu River, forced Carleton to evacuate Montreal, and nearly captured the governor in the process. Montgomery also largely destroyed the only two British regiments in the St. Lawrence Valley, leaving most of the province under his control, except for the city of Quebec itself. Montgomery then spent several

Richard Montgomery, by Charles Willson Peale, possibly after an engraving 1784–86. Courtesy of Independence National Historical Park.

weeks reorganizing his army in Montreal. He also used this time to forward American diplomatic objectives. Promising the French Canadians religious freedom and protection against the British, Montgomery attempted to organize a provincial convention to select delegates to the Continental Congress. Before this was accomplished, however, he proceeded against Quebec on November 28 with three hundred soldiers and some artillery, believing that the *habitants* would not embrace the American cause until the British had been defeated.[11]

While Montgomery's army operated in the Montreal area, a second American force commanded by Colonel Benedict Arnold moved against Quebec City through the Maine wilderness. The Americans hoped that Arnold could take the city with little resistance, as most of the British strength in Canada was deployed against Montgomery. Leaving Cambridge, Massachusetts, on September 13, Arnold led eleven hundred men up the Kennebec and Dead rivers, crossed the mountains, and then descended the

*Colonel Benedict Arnold, with Quebec in the
background. Courtesy of the Library of Congress.*

Chaudière River to the St. Lawrence near Pointe Lévy. Arnold's men faced
harsh weather and starvation during this horrific trek, which contemporaries
compared to Hannibal's march across the Alps. Nearly a third of Arnold's
men turned back or died en route, yet he reached the St. Lawrence by mid-
November, crossed the river, and unsuccessfully called for the city's surrender. Lacking the strength necessary to take Quebec, Arnold retreated about
twenty miles upriver to Pointe aux Trembles to await Montgomery. The two
American forces united on December 1, 1775, and then proceeded to lay siege
to Quebec, the last major British outpost in Canada.[12]

Throughout December, Montgomery repeatedly tried to get Carleton to
surrender the city, but to no avail. He sent messages to Quebec's merchants,
urging them to force the governor to capitulate before their property was
destroyed. Montgomery also bombarded Quebec but lacked powerful
artillery to breach its battlements. Faced with expiring enlistments among
Arnold's troops, Montgomery tried to storm the city in a howling blizzard
early on the morning of December 31. The attack turned into a fiasco. The

Americans lost 48 killed, including Montgomery and five other officers; 34 wounded, including Arnold; and 372 taken prisoners. The British losses were light: 5 dead and 14 wounded, only one of which proved serious. Although not apparent at the time, the assault's repulse effectively ended the American bid to seize Canada.[13] Despite the defeat, Arnold and later Generals David Wooster and John Thomas maintained the siege of Quebec through the spring.[14] They established outposts around the city and across the St. Lawrence at Pointe Lévy and tried to starve Quebec into submission.

The Baby journal demonstrates that the Americans received significant assistance from the French Canadians throughout the invasion. While the seigneurs and the clergy solidly backed the British, the same could not be said for the *habitants*. Men from sixteen parishes in the Quebec district alone enlisted with the invaders. How many *habitants* served with the Americans overall is difficult to determine, and it varied at different points during the year. Approximately three hundred armed *habitants* led by James Livingston, an Old Subject, awaited Montgomery's troops when they entered the province in September.[15] Others joined them as the Americans enjoyed military success. Armed Canadians intercepted British supplies, erected and manned a battery during the siege of St. Jeans, helped capture Fort Chambly, and participated in the operations against Quebec. In March, Benedict Arnold reported, "The inhabitants are generally in our favor, and many of them have taken up arms for us, or rather, for themselves." Congress eventually authorized raising two Canadian regiments, both of which continued to serve in the lower colonies after the invasion's collapse.[16]

The Baby journal reveals that some *habitants* suppressed royalist sentiments and urged their compatriots to support the Americans. For example, nine men from St. Pierre des Becquets terrorized the loyalist militia captain of Ste. Anne, Louis Gouin. They threatened to burn Gouin's house and forced him to give them money, weapons, and provisions. In St. Fereol, Beaumont, and St. Nicolas, *habitants* apprehended loyalists who attempted to travel to Quebec or otherwise assist the British. Clément Gosselin, an especially strong American partisan from Ste. Anne, "traveled to all of the others [parishes] as far as Pointe Lévy, preaching rebellion everywhere, inciting people to loot the small number of loyalists and have them arrested." In a number of cases, parishioners verbally abused or even arrested priests who seemed too zealous in supporting the crown. They also took advantage of the invasion as an excuse to settle old scores against the seigneurs by ransacking their estates. In the most extreme case, on March 25, 1776, men from seven parishes assisted an American detachment in routing a loyalist militia that was assembling at St. Pierre du Sud. Seven loyalists were killed, two were wounded, and thirty-eight made prisoners as *habitant* fought *habitant*.[17] Some of these men were even from the same parish, yet they fought on different sides.

In some parishes, women were the most zealous supporters of the Americans. Carleton's emissaries specifically identified four women for their subversive activities and in another case authorized the arrest of people, including women, who spoke against the government. These "Queens of Hungary," as the *habitants* nicknamed such women, held meetings to encourage American support and urged their neighbors to resist the British.[18] A widow in St. Vallier "caused more trouble in this parish than anyone" and served *habitants* strong drinks to further her efforts. The wife of Etienne Parant, the militia captain at Ste. Marie parish in Nouvelle Beauce, was cited for corrupting her husband. Although he had loyally supported the king previously, Parant openly admitted to letting American spies pass through his district during the invasion.

Most French Canadians who assisted the Americans did so in less dramatic but equally important ways, as the Baby journal makes clear. Fourteen parishes performed some type of corvée for the invaders, usually under their local militia officers' leadership. A feudal labor obligation, corvée involved maintaining the roads, transporting goods, or doing some other type of public service. For example, *habitants* in St. Henry built ladders for the invaders as corvée.[19] Besides corvée, other *habitants* gathered firewood and assisted the Americans in building and maintaining a series of signal fires. The invaders established these fires below Quebec to provide a warning when a British relief fleet arrived in the St. Lawrence. Many *habitants* sold the Americans provisions, including to Arnold's starving troops when they first entered Canada.[20] On the rebels' orders, the *habitants* in a number of parishes also elected new militia officers, undermining British authority.

Despite the various forms of assistance that they provided the invaders, in the end, most Canadians did not do any more than this and failed to flock to support the Americans. The Baby journal notes that in many cases, *habitants* assisted the Americans only because of fear or against their will. Others did so "without resistance" but not necessarily with eagerness. This was because the invaders could not keep the promises that they had made to the *habitants* or guarantee their future protection. Examples of some of these American failings are evident in the Baby journal.

Throughout the campaign, the Americans lacked sufficient specie to purchase provisions. Over time, the shortage became more acute, and they were increasingly forced to pay the *habitants* with paper scrip. History exacerbated this problem. During the Seven Years' War, the French government had issued a similar currency, which caused ruinous inflation and was ultimately repudiated. When the Americans resorted to this tactic, it brought back many bad memories and undermined their claims of respecting private property. Even worse, on March 4 Arnold took the dramatic step of requiring the Canadians near Quebec to accept paper currency on fear of being treated as "an Enemy of the united Colonies." By spring 1776, the invaders even lacked enough of this and resorted to requisitioning supplies. The Baby journal notes several cases where Canadians enlisted or provided the rebels with services or supplies but were never paid. A further example of this was found in Cap Santé, where the *habitants* "willingly delivered provisions to the rebels' camp as long as they were paid in money." In Montreal, American troops confiscated merchandise from shops and gave their owners receipts. Throughout the campaign, Montgomery and other American officers worried about using paper money and suggested methods to make it more acceptable to the Canadians.[21] These efforts failed, however, with extremely detrimental effects for the Americans.

The British took advantage of the money situation to further discredit the invaders. On October 5, 1775, a letter published in the *Quebec Gazette* stated, "Can you think, that these people who are without food and ammunition will allow you to enjoy peacefully the fruits of your labors, no; they will take your grain, your cattle and everything that you have . . . and they will pay you with notes; (which they call Province Bills, or Bills of Credit) what will you do with such money? nothing."[22] By March, the British garrison at Quebec began to receive reports that the *habitants* would no longer accept the paper currency, which accounts for Arnold's decision. One militia officer wrote that the French Canadians "are glad to exchange a handful of it for a dollar."[23]

Connecticut general David Wooster's administration of Montreal further hurt the American cause. Wooster, the garrison commander and second ranking officer behind Montgomery, interfered with property even more by refusing to issue fur trade licenses, believing that they benefited pro-British Indians. He also allowed his strong Puritan heritage to become a factor by restricting Catholicism, despite Congress's and Montgomery's promises to the contrary. Most notably, he ordered churches closed on Christmas Eve, which angered many *habitants*. The Americans arrested three Récollet friars from Trois Rivières for violating one of Wooster's pronouncements against speaking favorably of the British. In spring 1776, Congress tried to rectify the deteriorating situation in Canada by sending a delegation there. It included the Catholic Marylander Charles Carroll and his cousin, Father John Carroll. This mission arrived far too late, however, and did little to restore American claims of toleration.

Wooster further undercut the American position when he ordered the arrest of suspected loyalists and confiscated weapons in several suburbs. Some of these individuals were later released, but not before the Canadians turned over several hostages to the Americans to ensure their good behavior. While some of these actions were justified, Wooster's heavy-handed methods did little to make the Canadians believe that the Americans had come to bring "Liberty and Security," not "oppression and violence." When the congressional committee issued its report, it blamed Wooster for many of the problems in Canada and urged his removal.[24]

The obvious weakness of the American army in Canada further underscored the other problems of the American occupation and diminished the *habitants'* confidence in the invaders. While the invaders had enjoyed victory in the latter half of 1775, this changed after the disastrous December 31 assault on Quebec. Desertions, expiring enlistments, and a severe outbreak of small-pox further decimated American strength and undercut the reinforcements that arrived in the province. By late March, Arnold reported that at Quebec he could field only approximately five hundred men.[25]

While the invaders' strength ebbed, Canadian loyalists became more active, as evidenced by their gathering at St. Pierre du Sud. Meanwhile, loy-alists in Montreal gathered guns and munitions to assist a British-Indian force moving against the city from Oswegatchie on the upper St. Lawrence. One American officer clearly recognized the *habitants*' changing sentiments when he wrote that they were "no longer . . . friends, but, on the contrary, waiting an opportunity to join our enemies." The arrival of British ships, loaded with reinforcements, at Quebec on May 6 settled the issue once and for all. Carleton ordered an immediate sortie, and the besieging army fled, abandoning large amounts of equipment and stores. Although the Americans managed to maintain a presence in Canada for another six weeks, their occu-pation of the province was clearly at an end.[26]

On May 18, the British and Indian force from Oswegatchie surrounded four hundred Americans at the Cedars, forty miles west of Montreal, and convinced them to surrender the next day. On May 19, the British and Indi-ans ambushed a relief column heading for the Cedars and took another one hundred prisoners before returning to Oswegatchie, when Arnold approached with a large force. Meanwhile, the main American army contin-ued to retreat from Quebec. After briefly halting at Deschambault, it contin-ued to fall back to Sorel and then St. Jeans on the Richelieu River by May 30. There it was reinforced to nearly seven thousand men commanded by General John Sullivan.[27] Receiving a report that only eight hundred British and Canadian troops held Trois Rivières, Sullivan dispatched General William Thompson and two thousand troops to counterattack.[28] Thompson left on June 6 and arrived early in the morning two days later but became hopelessly lost in the forests and swamps near Trois Rivières. By the time the Americans managed to find the town, Carleton's main force had arrived. It easily repulsed the American attack, killing 50 and capturing 236 others, including Thompson. British losses were eight dead and nine wounded.[29]

*L'Honorable François Baby, by Lt. Col. A.-D.
Aubry. Courtesy of the National Archives of
Canada (C-8852).*

This defeat, coupled with that at the Cedars, convinced Sullivan that Canada was lost. He resumed the retreat with his ragged, smallpox-infested army, and the last American troops left Canada by the end of June.[30]

With the Americans in retreat, Carleton created a commission to reestablish the militia that had performed so poorly and had seen many of its officers assist the invaders. He also charged his envoys with investigating who had collaborated with the Americans. For the Quebec and Trois Rivières region, the governor selected François Baby, Gabriel-Elzéar Taschereau, and Jenkin Williams, three men who represented both the French Canadians and Old Subjects.[31]

François Baby (1733–1820) was a prominent merchant and fur trader who had fought against the British during the Seven Years' War. Following the war, he resumed his commercial interests and established ties to London merchants. More importantly, Baby reconciled himself to British rule. In 1773, he presented a petition in London from Canadian merchants and seigneurs that helped lay the basis for the Quebec Act. Baby also became a close friend and confidant of Carleton and Frederick Haldimand, who became governor in 1778.[32] Baby served as a captain in the Quebec militia during the American invasion and was appointed adjutant general of the militia and commissary of military transportation in 1776. He held these positions until 1811 and 1812, respectively. The most influential of Carleton's three envoys, he later served on Quebec's Executive and Legislative councils. Baby was the Speaker of the latter in 1791, 1802–3, and 1806–7.[33]

Gabriel-Elzéar Taschereau (1745–1809) was the seigneur of Ste. Marie-de-la-Nouvelle Beauce. Like Baby, he initially opposed British rule but quickly adjusted to the new order, as did most seigneurs. In May 1775, Taschereau unsuccessfully tried to raise the militia in St. Joseph-de-la-Nouvelle Beauce, and he later participated in repulsing the American assault on Quebec on December 31. As one of Carleton's envoys in spring 1776, Taschereau had a vested interest in the investigation, as the Baby journal makes clear. *Habitants* had ransacked his estate at Ste. Marie, auctioned his possessions, and seized money from him.[34]

Jenkin Williams (1734–1819), the sole Englishman on the commission, was a successful lawyer who settled in Canada in 1767. In this regard, he represented the recently arrived Old Subjects. Williams served as the register of the Court of Chancery and was one of the commissioners who replaced Quebec's chief justice during his absence in 1773.[35]

Between May 22 and July 18, at which point the Baby journal abruptly ends, the three men visited fifty-six parishes and missions, reviewing at least 4,041 militiamen.[36] At each parish, the commissioners dismissed disloyal officers, appointed new ones, and wrote a general summary of the *habitants'* role during the invasion. The main punishment meted out to disloyal subjects was loss of military rank and, in some cases, public humiliation. In fourteen parishes, the commissioners banned a total of sixty-two men from ever holding a government commission again.[37] In most other cases, however, they urged the *habitants* to recognize their loyalty to Britain and had them shout "Long live the King." This mild yet firm response proved

*Judge Gabriel-Elzéar Taschereau. Courtesy of the
National Archives of Canada (C-92935).*

effective, and no other major disruptions occurred in Canada during the American Revolution.

Baby and his colleagues attempted to relieve the severe logistical problem that plagued British forces in Canada by urging the *habitants* to carry their goods to Quebec. The commissioners repeatedly enjoined them to maintain the roads as a way of facilitating the transportation of troops and supplies. Following the six-month blockade, Quebec's garrison was low on provisions. Even after they retreated in May 1776, the Americans contributed to the shortage by stripping the region of grain and livestock to maintain their forces. A British relief fleet that arrived that spring helped alleviate the problem, but one of its four supply ships sank en route. Additional ships ultimately brought provisions for twelve thousand troops to Canada, but nearly twenty thousand people needed to be fed by the time militia, Indians, and civilian auxiliaries were included. Carleton's forces also lacked enough tarps and tents to cover their supplies, so some were destroyed by the weather or careless handling. To rectify this situation, the British resorted to buying provisions from the *habitants*, hence the call to carry goods to Quebec and maintain the roads. Between June 1776 and January 1777, Carleton's commissary general, Nathaniel Day, purchased £70,000 of meat, flour, bread, and other provisions from the Canadians.[38]

In retrospect, American success in Canada depended upon their winning the *habitants*' support. The Americans tried to accomplish this by appealing to rights, property, and religious toleration, all reinforced by military success. The Baby journal demonstrates that they made some headway, as evidenced by the many *habitants*, including women, who espoused their cause and assisted them in various ways. Many *habitants* were not this committed, however. The Baby journal reports that while some Canadians embraced the invaders enthusiastically, others did so "without opposition" or against their will. This illustrates that many *habitants* wished to remain neutral in a war between English-speaking peoples, and they supported whoever held the upper hand. When the Americans proved unable to protect Canadian property, religion, or security, most *habitants* abandoned any attachments they had for them. The Baby journal helps explain why this occurred. It provides a detailed view of a people caught in a war not of their own making, and it reveals how they responded.

Abbreviations
found in the Baby Journal

Alexdre . . . . . Alexandre
Augn . . . . . . Augustin
Augusn . . . . . Augustin
Bapte . . . . . . Baptiste
Bone . . . . . . Boniface
Bte . . . . Baptiste
Capt. . . . . . . Captain
Chas . . . . . . Charles
Chs . . . . Charles
Clémt . . . . . . Clément
commissn . . . commission
do . . . . ditto
Ense . . . . . . Ensign
Franc . . . . . . François
Frans . . . . . . François
Gab. . . . . . . Gabriel
Gabril . . . . . Gabriel
Genl Carln . . General Carleton
Gouvr . . . . . Governor
habt . . . . *habitant*
hble . . . . Honorable
Jacqs . . . . Jacques
Jaq. . . . . Jacques
J. Bte . . . . . . Jean Baptiste

Jn Bte . . . . . . Jean Baptiste
Jos. . . . . Joseph
Josh . . . . Joseph
Lieut . . . . . . Lieutenant
Lieut Col. . . Lieutenant Colonel
Lt Gouvr . . . Lieutenant Governor
M. . . . . Monsieur
Mad. . . . . . . Madam
Messrs . . . . . Messieurs
Mich. . . . . . . Michel
Monseigr . . . Monsignor
Monsr . . . . . Monsieur
Mr . . . . Monsieur
Mrs . . . . Messieurs
Nbre . . . . . . November
Pre . . . . Pierre
Pte . . . . Pointe
Revd . . . . . . Reverend
Serg. . . . . Sergeants
Sergt . . . . . . Sergeant
Sergts . . . . . Sergeants
St . . . . Saint
Ste . . . . .Sainte

Journal

By Messrs Frans Baby, Gab. Taschereau, and Jenkin Williams
during the tour they took in the district of Quebec
by order of General Carleton for the establishment of militias
in each parish and for the examination of people who have assisted
or aided the rebels of whom we have taken note.

Curé M: Desroches   Mecredy 22 may

a une heure apres midy partis de Quebec

Vieille Lorette

Point d'officiers de Milice d'établis, ayant refusé d'en
Mecredy   recevoir l'année dernière.
22.   Donné ordre au Baillif pour une Revue general
          Jeudy 23 may, a sept heures du matin,
          apres la lecture des Commissions,
          Passé la milice en Revue, établie en bon ordre. 160 hom.
          Nommés pour Officiers, et fait reconnaître par la lecture
          des commissions.
          Antoine, Huotine, Capt.
          Ch.ᵉ Noreau, Lieuten.t } Commissionés le 22 may
          Antoine Folin Enseigne.
          Ignace Gougy.
Jeudy   Joseph, Allin —
23.   Prisques, Mathieu } Sergents
          André, Robitaille.
          Arrangée pour leur faire connaître la commission envers le
Souvenir Donné ordre au Capitaine de faire un Rôle exact
          et l'Indignation des fidels Sujets contre ceux qui ont aidés les
Rebels   de Sa Compagnie et d'y distinguer les âges au dessus de
          cinquante cinq ans a Soixante et 16 — a 55. aussi
          les Garçons d'avec les peres de familles et de nous
          l'envoyer en Ville au plustôt. apres la Revue faite
          on a crié trois fois Vive le Roy avec applaudissement
          nous leur avons recommandé de porter leurs armés
          en Ville avec asurance.

*The journal of François Baby, Gabriel Taschereau, and Jenkin Williams. Courtesy of the
University of Montreal.*

Left Quebec at 1:00 P.M.

Vieille Lorette

Parish priest, Mr [Ignace] Desroches.[1]

No militia officers appointed; they had refused to receive any last year.

Wednesday, [May] 22.

Ordered the bailiff to call a general review.[2]

Thursday, May 23 at 7:00 A.M.

After the reading of our charges. Reviewed 160 men, appointed officers, and officially read their commissions:

Antoine Riverin, Capt.
Chs Noreau, Lieutenant   appointed May 22.
Ignace Govin, Ensign
Joseph Allin ⎫
Prisques Mathieu ⎬   Sergeants
André Robitaille ⎭

Arranged for the public submission to their Sovereign and [expressed] his loyal subjects' indignation against those who assisted the rebels. We ordered the captain to take an exact count of his company and to separate men above fifty-five to sixty years old from those 16 to 55, likewise unmarried men from heads of families and to send it to us quickly. After the review, we cheered, "Long live the King" three times with enthusiasm. We have recommended that the people bring forth their goods to the town [Quebec] with assurances [of safety].

This parish, for the most part, did not take up arms for the rebels but provided them with fire and kindling wood, in obedience to their orders. Only three young men took it upon themselves to go to the rebels' camp with their arms, but having been well advised otherwise, they returned home having been made aware of their mistake.

. Cited as disloyal subjects, Plamondon, the father, and Plamondon, his son, land-surveyors, and the tall Pierre Drollet, who had been advised not to receive any government officers. The said Plamondon and his son stirred the *habitants* in favor of the rebels, always assuring them that Quebec would fall, and that the royalists would not receive any reinforcements; Garneau, a farmer for le sieur Dupon and a strong rebel partisan, incited his countrymen to loot.

Left at 11:00 A.M. for Jeune Lorette.

Jeune Lorette

Missionary for the Indians, Father [Etienne-Thomas de Villeneuve] Girou [Girault].

No militia officers were appointed last fall since they refused to receive any from the government.

Thursday [May], 23.

The militia assembled at 4:00 P.M.

The reading of our charges.

Appointment of the officers and the reading of their commissions:

Joseph Barbau, Captain
François Barbau, Lieutenant May 23

View of Jeune Lorette, the village of the Hurons, nine miles north of Quebec, by George Heriot. Courtesy of the National Archives of Canada (C-11065).

Jacques Barbau }
Louis Lureux } Sergeants

Reviewed 55 men and the rest as of this morning.

This company did not take up arms against the government, but most of the people carried out the rebels' orders to provide them with fire and kindling wood.

Left at 6:00 P.M. for Charle[s]bourg.

Charle[s]bourg

Parish priest, Mr [François] Borel.

No militia officers were appointed last fall since they had refused to accept any from the government.

Friday, May 24.

The militia assembled at 7:00 A.M.

The reading of our charges.

Appointment of officers and the reading of their commissions:

Jacques Jobin, Capt.	Charle[s]bourg's Company
Jean Trudel, Lieut	Appointed on May 22.
Pierre Jaq. Jobin ⎫	
Pierre Lefevre ⎬ Sergeants	
Jean A. Bedard ⎭	
Raphael Giroux, Capt.	Bourg Royal's Company
Jean Bte Belanger, Lieut	Appointed on May 24
Jean Parady ⎫	
~~Dominique Coty~~ ⎬ Sergeants	
François Lavigneur ⎭	

Reviewed 250 men and the rest as of May 23 & c.

François Breton, a baker residing in Charle[s]bourg, is accused by the three above-mentioned parishes of having helped the rebels in all manners. He employed all sorts of methods to corrupt his countrymen and, notably, attempted to form a company.

Jacques Allard cited for having proclaimed himself captain in the rebels' service and, consequently, for having carried out their orders.

Germain Thibaut. The same serving as Jacques Allard's sergeant.

Louis Pasquet cited for having incited the *habitants* to take up arms for the rebels.

Louis Joseph Geobin, the son, cited for having taken up arms and denouncing his priest to the rebels.

Charles Delonais took up arms and made seditious remarks.

The two Canards or [and?] Renaud du Gropin seditiously refused to be appointed [as] government officers and invited their countrymen to do the same.

The same: Pierre Parent from Petit Village.

François Falardeau, Breton's son-in-law, cited for having made an allegation against his priest and for acting in concert with his father-in-law's [activities] against the government.

On January 1, several young men from St Pierre Village, after having had several drinks, voluntarily left with their arms to aid the rebels. Most of them returned home, not having gone half way, and the others went as far as the General Hospital.[3] They returned home the following day without having done anything.

This parish, with the exception of those above-mentioned, did not take up arms against the government. The majority of the people obeyed the rebels' orders to provide them with fire and kindling wood.

Left for Beauport at 1:00 P.M.

Beauport

Parish priest, Mr [Pierre-Simon] Renaud [Renauld].

Saturday, May 25.

The militia assembled at 8:00 A.M.

The reading of our charges.

Appointment of officers and the reading of their commissions:

Paul Rainville, Capt.	appointed on May 24
Jean Garnau, Lieut	
François Allard	
Jacques Louis Parant	
Joseph Maheu	Sergeants
Joseph Girou	
Pierre Latouche	

Reviewed 150 men.

Public address. [Cheered] "Long live the King," the rest as routine & c.

Ordered them to put the King's wood [that was] found on beaches in a safe place and to notify the Lt Gouvr [Hector Cramahé] that they had done so.[4]

Thanks [for loyal service] and dismissal of old Captain Pre Maillou, only on account of his great age.

Cashiered and withdrew the government commissions of the said Jean Vallé, lieut, and André Marcoux, ensign, for having submitted to the rebels' orders out of fear.

Pierre Parant, capt., was appointed by the rebels' congress. Charles Girou enrolled his two sons, Benjamin and Louis Girou, in the rebels' service for 40 # per month.[5] Louis Binet did the same with his son. Both urged these young men to go help the rebels in their camp on the day of the assault, December 31.[6]

Pierre Duprat served under Captain Pre Parant in the rank of sergeant for them [the rebels].

Louis Galarnaux, a married man, enrolled in the rebels' service.

Louis Maheu, ditto.

The widow Jean Marcoux's son and a few others from this parish did the same.

Alexandre Vallé shouted at the church doors in front of the *habitants* that they should go help the rebels if they could not take the town [Quebec].

Gautier, a cobbler, wickedly pledged in front of a certain Reigné de Roussi, a rebel officer, that les sieurs Larche and [Jean] Garnau [Garneau] had spent their efforts inciting the people of Ile d'Orléans to side with the town.[7] Finally, most of the *habitants* of this parish stood guard and assisted the rebels in various ways.

Left for L'Ange Gardien at 10:00 A.M.

[L']Ange Gardien

Parish priest, Mr [Joseph-Romain] Dolbec.[8]

Saturday, May 25.

The militia assembled at 4:00 P.M.

The reading of our charges.

Appointment of the officers and the reading of their commissions:

Michel Huot, capt., appointed by His Excellency [Sir Guy Carleton] on July 7, 1775, was reinstated for having conducted himself as a faithful subject. We commissioned Philippe Trudel, lieutenant, on May 25.

Simon Lecomte } Sergeants
Mathurin Huot }

Reviewed 70 men.

Public addresses. [Cheered] "Long live the King" & c.

Ordered them to put the King's wood [that was] found on beaches in a safe place and to notify the Lieut Governor that they had done so.

Cashiered and withdrew the commissions given by the governor to Louis Goulet, lieutenant, and to Chs Cantin, ensign, for having served the rebels most willingly.

Nicolas Lecomte is accused of having requested a captain's commission from the rebels, of having proclaimed the said appointment throughout the parish, and of having acted harshly in this rank throughout the winter. He had the said Capt. Michel Huot disarmed. He also had the named Guillaume Hébert, Prisque Cantin, Joseph Huot, Ignace Canté, and Simon Lecomte disarmed by the rebels for having refused to obey their orders. He had several *habitants'* oxen requisitioned. Finally, he used all the means in his power to prove his sympathy to the rebels. As a result of the above information, we had the said [Le]Comte brought to us to swear in front of the whole parish that he had burned the said commission. We declared the said Lecomte unworthy and barred him from ever holding any position for the government or the parish until the general's will is known. We announced that if the said Lecomte had not already burned his commission himself, we would have ordered the executioner to do it publicly.

The above-mentioned Capt. Michel Huot declared that only 18 parishioners, whose names he could not give with certainty, served the rebels willingly, and that the rest had been coerced.

Left for Château [Richer] at 5:00 P.M.

Château Riche[r]⁹

Ministered by Ste Anne's parish priest.

Sunday, May 26.

The militia assembled at 8:00 A.M.

The reading of our charges.

We withdrew the captain's commission given by His Excellency to the said Ustache Bâcon, who appears to have been coerced to serve the rebels in his rank.

We acted in the same manner towards le sieur Zachary Cloutier for the same reasons. After having searched to no avail for some *habitants* of this parish deserving of the honor to serve the King, we voiced our outrage in front of the militia and postponed the appointment of officers until the following Tuesday, [May] 28, at 9:00 A.M. We have retained the bailiffs in their positions until that time.

Departed for Ste Anne at 10:00 A.M.

Ste Anne

Parish priest, Mr [Jean-François] Hubert.¹⁰

The militia assembled at 4:00 P.M.

The reading of our charges.

Thanks to le sieur Chevalier for his loyalty to the King. We offered him the captain's commission, if he wished to leave his roadmender trade, which he graciously declined.

Cashiered Bonaventure Lessard, appointed by His Excellency last fall, because he served in the rank of captain for the rebels. It seems that he was forced to do so.

Cashiered Jean Paré, appointed captain of St Féréol last fall by His Excellency General Carleton, although he never accepted the said commission.

Appointed officers:

Augustin Symarre, Capt.

Jn Bte Racine *dit* Noyer, Lieut

Frans Lessard ⎤

Joseph Giguère ⎦   Sergeants

For St Féréol

Ministered by Ste Anne's parish priest.

Prisque Paré, Capt.

No lieutenant due to the small size of the company.

Joseph Gagnon, Sergeant

Discharge of the bailiffs.

Sunday, May 26.

Public address to urge submission to the Sovereign. [Cheered] "Long live the King." The rest as usual & c.

Augustin Lacroix incited several young men from this parish to join the rebels. He stood guard at Sault, always talking of sedition.[11] He opposed the passage of St Joachim's *habitants* when they attempted to go offer their services to the governor last fall. In short, he was one of the most disloyal subjects in this parish.

Last fall, Chrétien Giguère refused the King's commission and encouraged others to do the same. He repeatedly boasted, at the church doors, of the rebels' strength and power in order to persuade [the people] that the town was very much threatened. It should be noted that this man is highly respected in this parish.

The three sons of a certain Augustin Cynard have stood guard and have reported the names of those who refused to do so to the rebels. Almost all the *habitants* of this parish stood guard at the Sault armed with rifles. Several young men loaded their rifles before leaving the village, swearing that they would fire on anyone who tried to pursue them.

This winter, Caron du Plaquet, *dit* Chevalier, the village roadmender, served at Ste Anne. He was the one who read all Congress's orders at the

A view of the Falls of the Montmorency with General Haldimand's country house near it, May 1, 1781, by James Peachey. Courtesy of the National Archives of Canada (C-2020).

church doors. He wrote answers to Congress on behalf of the parish's capt., a certain Bonaventure Lessare [Lessard], who had previously been appointed by the King. He visited the rebels' camp several times to bring them provisions and, when returning, assured those he met everywhere that rebel reinforcement had arrived and that their ranks already numbered over eleven thousand men. He helped spread the rumor that attempts to sortie from the town had resulted in a debacle. Once when the rebels had sounded an alarm at the General Hospital, he joined them, accompanied by a certain Lesperance from St Joachim, to fight the King's troops.

Left for St Joachim at 6:00 P.M.

St Joachim

Parish priest, Mr Corbin.

Monday, May 27.

The militia assembled at 8:00 A.M.

The reading of our charges.

Dismissal of Capt. Jean Trudel, commissioned by the King, for having given commands in the parish by orders of the rebels. We thanked him for having constantly refused to implement any of their orders. He declined any service in their favor, having even let the rebels disarm him by force, thus giving ample proof [that he was] a zealous servant of the King.

Public address to recommend good conduct from the majority of this parish.

Reprimanded those who sympathized with the rebels.

Discharge of the bailiffs.

Appointed as officers:

Joseph Paré, formerly Lieutenant, Capt.
François Fortin, Lieutenant
Guillaume Gosselin ⎫
                    ⎬ Sergeants
René Gagnon   ⎭

Reviewed 86 men.

The rest as usual, & c.

It must be noted that Capt. Joseph Paré showed such a zeal for the King during the winter that he suffered some mistreatment from the rebels.

The aforementioned Lesperance did all he could to help the rebels.[12] He preached rebellion in every parish he visited, including this one. He succeeded in forming a party and, thinking that the priest [Henri-François] Gravé and the vicar Corbin were interfering with his plans, had them brought to the rebels' camp.[13] In short, he had been appointed captain and, in that rank, placed himself at the rebels' disposal to have their orders carried out and to help them loot the priests' farms.

Pierre Alaire served the rebels as a major and, in this rank, oversaw guards and convoys in concert with Lesperance.

A few *habitants* of this parish stood guard once or twice, but afterwards almost all of them refused to do so.

The named Jean Marie Mercier, a young boy, enlisted with the rebels and served for two months on the promise of 40 # per month, which he never received.

Ten parishioners had been disarmed by a Canadian guard commanded by a *Bostonnais* officer guided by Lesperance.[14] These people [the parishioners] were suspected of readying themselves to join a group raised in the south by Monsr Baujeu [Beaujeu] in support of the town.[15]

Eight people were brought to the rebel sentries for having refused to stand guard at the Sault. The officer in command, after having threatened them, had them sent to the Beauport guard to force them to stand guard. To avoid having to comply, they bribed the guards with one piastre each and, once released, returned home.[16]

The next day 20 men went to the camp to find their priest, who had been taken prisoner. He was released, and they returned home.

The named Gravel, a cobbler and a shrewd, cunning individual, was very attached to the rebels but never compromised himself. He covertly prompted others on every occasion and encouraged those *habitants* whom he knew favored the Congress.

Left at 5:00 P.M. to return to Château [Richer].

Return to Château Riche[r]

Tuesday, May 28.

The militia assembled at 9:00 A.M.

Public address on the bad conduct of this parish.

Discharge of the bailiffs.

Appointment of the officers and the reading of their commissions:

Joseph Cazau, Capt.

Ignace Gravel, Lieut   May 28

François Poulin ⎫
Jean Toupin   ⎬ Sergeants

Reviewed 73 men. Cheered, "Long live the King" three times.

Pierre Gravel, an innkeeper and a close friend of Lesperance, used his house to hold meetings to foster the spirit of rebellion in the said parish and spoke scornfully of royalist leaders. He did not stand guard due to his old age, but his son did.

Chs Taillon and Jean Trepaigné, the principal opposition leaders in this parish during the establishment of the militia last fall and up to the last moment, have always voiced seditious comments. This allowed the *habitants* to hope that Quebec would soon fall.

On December 8, the said Trepaigné told Dug[g]an that there was some salt [stored] at one of the priests' farms. [The salt] belonged to a bourgeois from Quebec.[17]

The entire parish, with the exception of the old men, stood guard at Sault during the winter. A great number seem to have done so most willingly and the rest without much resistance.

Crossed [the St Lawrence] to Ste Famille, Ile d'Orléans, at 10:00 A.M.

Ile D'Orléans Ste Famille Parish

Parish priest, M. [Gilles] Udau [Eudo].

Tuesday, May 28.

The militia assembled at 4:00 P.M.

The reading of our charges.

Appointment of the officers and the reading of their commissions:

Jacques Perraut, Capt.
Pre Deblois *dit* Germain, Lieut   May 28
Etienne Frouin, Pierre's son ⎤
Etienne Giguère   ⎥
Augustin Bauché   ⎬ Sergeants
Jacques Pichet   ⎦

Reviewed 120 men, public address, [Cheered] "Long live the King" & c.
Called forth and had Bazil Bauché *dit* Morancy brought to us in front of

the said militia. Ordered [that] a lantern be brought to us and forced the said Bauché to turn in the captain's commission that he had received from the rebels. After having read it publicly, we forced him to burn it with his own hand, telling him sarcastically that for lack of a public executioner he would have to serve as his own. This punishment seems to have made a strong impression on all present.

The said Bazil Bauché Morancy is accused, although indirectly, of being a strong partisan of the rebels and of having sergeants under his command act with vigilance. With the assistance of Bte Lognon, he has enlisted the parish to stand guard at the end of the island. He threatened to burn Captain Perrault's property because he ordered his children to join the King's service.

Joseph Leureau constantly voiced seditious comments and supplied provisions to the rebels.

Baptiste Grancham *dit* Cornelier, a seditious man, boasted that he made sixty trips to the rebels' camp and, because of his actions, they appointed his father-in-law, Bazil Bauché Morancy, captain.

One day after leaving Mass, he [Baptiste Grancham *dit* Cornelier] shouted in front of Reigné de Roussy [Roussi], one of Congress's officer, "I declare that I believe that Prémont and myself are the only true friends of the Congress in this parish." He went to St François parish to tell its *habitants* that the people of Ste Famille were ready to stand guard for the rebels and that since the said Reigné de Roussi would soon arrive to order them to do so, he advised that they not refuse.

Mr Prémont served as Bauché Morancy's sergeant. So did Ignace Avare who, this last [winter] led thirty young men to the end of the island where they stood guard. He stayed with them for eight days and relentlessly tried to convince them that no relief would come for the town. In short, he greatly contributed to corrupting this parish.

Last fall, Drouin Lemaine refused to accept a capt.'s commission for the King. On the threat that the parish would be burned if he could not provide 15 young men to go to Montreal, he arrogantly retorted, "We'll be waiting for you."[18] He proceeded to encourage the parish to resist. He went to St Pierre with all those that he could find. There, they also found some people from

St François. He left with a detachment to go stand guard at the end of the island in order to resist the town's actions if it tried to burn the opposing parishes.

A certain number [of people] from this parish tried all they could to remain good royalists.

Slept in Ste Famille and left for St François at 7:00 A.M.

St François—Ile D'Orléans

Parish priest, Mr [François] Guarne [Le Guerne].[19]

Wednesday, May 29.

The militia assembled at 10:00 A.M.

The reading of our charges.

Appointment of the officers and the reading of their commissions:

Joseph Lepage, Capt.

Jacques Guérard, Lieut   Commissioned on May 29

Louis Pépin, the son of Louis ⎫

Joseph Drouin   ⎭ Sergeants

Reviewed 70 men.

Public address, [Cheered] "Long live the King" & c.

Discharge of the bailiffs.

Dismissal of Jean Plante, Joseph Belouin, and Jean Labbé, commissioned by the government this fall, for having stood guard for the rebels or [having] forced others to do so.

Called forth and had Louis Pépin, *dit* Major, brought to us. In front of the whole said militia, we told him that we knew that he had received a militia captain's commission given to him by the rebels. We were sure that he had only accepted this commission out of fear and weakness because previously he had always demonstrated obedience to his King. Nevertheless, we condemned him for having had the baseness of accepting this commission and, in the absence of a public executioner, had him burn it with his own hand.

The sentence was read in a loud and ironic tone in the presence of the entire militia of this parish.

Jean Acelin did everything possible for the rebels in order to get a militia captain's commission for the said parish. He succeeded and was appointed. This commission was then transferred to the said Louis Pépin on the demand of a great number of the *habitants* who refused to accept the said Acelin. He had previously received command of 50 men, and he had ruled them harshly and with too great a zeal on behalf of the rebels.

The said Jean Acelin, Jean Marçau, Big Collet, Jean Labbé, lieut, were dismissed. Augustin Marçau and Michel Hemond have always fomented trouble and are the most disloyal subjects in this parish. They formed a party of revolutionaries and, last fall, marched to the end of the island to oppose the government's orders to appoint new officers.

A group from this parish stood guard, others refused to do so.

Left at 2:00 P.M. for St Jean.

St Jean—Ile D'Orléans

Parish priest, Mr [Pierre] Mennard.

Wednesday, May 29.

The militia assembled at 4:00 P.M.

The reading of our charges.

Appointment of the officers and the reading of their commissions:

Louis Genais *dit* Labarre, Capt.	May 29	
Franc Pépin *dit* Lachance, Lieut		
Joseph Blanchard ⎱	Sergeants	
J. Bte Deroussel ⎰		

Reviewed 110 men.

Discharge of the bailiffs.

Dismissal of Joseph Blouin, capt., Laurent Genais *dit* Labarre, capt.-assistant, Laurent Tivierge, lieut, and Guillaume Audi *dit* Lapointe, ensign, for having stood guard at the end of the island for the rebels. The above-mentioned Capt. Joseph Blouin [was dismissed] only for having warned the *habitants* to follow the rebels' orders in an ill-conceived political move. However, we know that he refused to accept commissions from the rebels, whom he despised, and that on all other occasions he acted as a true and faithful subject of the King.

Jean Hemont accepted a capt.'s commission from the rebels and Joseph Plante that of lieutenant. Both of them have sworn in front of the said militia (upon our demand that they produce their alleged commissions given by the rebels) that they had burned them three weeks prior to our arrival. We told them that they had done exactly what we wished and that we could not begin to express the scorn and outrage that such appointments deserved. We made them serve as their own executioner in front of the whole parish, as we had done in other parishes. We declared the said Jean Hemont and Joseph Plante unworthy and barred them from ever holding any other position in the King's name or in the parish's service. We ordered the parishioners to bar them from participating in any assembly of any kind.

The said Capt. Jean Hemont carried out his orders forcefully with much authority to prove his zeal and made several trips to the rebels' camp.

Joseph Plante, his lieut, was even more disloyal as witnessed by his seditious remarks and the arrogance of his commands.

Etienne Dalaire, 68 years old, had initially accepted a commission from the rebels, which he later resigned in favor of Jean Hemond [Hemont].

Pierre Gagné, Jean Marie Tivierge, Antoine Gobeille, the son of Berthelmy, and the above-mentioned men are the most disloyal subjects in this parish. Last fall they led a group of 20 to 25 men to the end of the island to oppose the government's orders.

It seems that Laurent Genais *dit* Labarre, previously mentioned, acted wrongly out of weakness and fear, having declared since that he would rather be burned alive than help the rebels or any of the dismissed officers.

Everyone, with the exception of the newly appointed officers, had stood guard last winter, most of them willingly, although a few parishioners did refuse to go when ordered to do so.

Jacques Tramblé and François Louverdière served the rebels in the rank of sergeant.

Louis Hemond [Hemont], as disloyal a subject as his brother, capt. of the rebels, delivered a large amount of flour to their camp. Several others did the same without being forced.

Left on Thursday, May 30, at 7:00 A.M. for St Laurent.

St Laurent—Ile D'Orléans

Ministered by Mr [Alexis] Pinet, Monsignor [Louis-Philippe] Desgly's [D'Esgly] vicar.[20]

Thursday, May 30.

The militia assembled at 9:00 A.M.

The reading of our charges.

Dismissal of the following commissioned by the King:

Marc Dufrêne, Capt.

Guillaume Sinmar, Lieut

Antoine Chabot, Ensign

For reasons we shall give later.

Discharge of the bailiffs.

Shaming of the *habitants* of this parish because almost all stood guard [for the rebels].

Appointment of the officers:

Louis Roulau, Capt.

Pierre Labrie, Lieut

Frans Rouillé ⎤

Antoine Couture ⎬ Sergeants

François Ruel ⎦

Invitation to the *habitants* to bring their goods to town & c. [Cheered]

"Long live the King" & c.

Reviewed 96 men.

The officers that we dismissed had served the rebels in their respective rank.

Le sieur Marc Dufrêne shouted at the church doors that those who would not obey Congress's orders would be looted. In other words, he always showed a great zeal and sympathy for the rebels.

Last fall, Joseph Fortier did all he could to prevent Louis Roulau from accepting a commission in the King's service, telling him that the general did not have the right to issue such orders.

Laurent Audet *dit* Lapointe and Louis Colombe went to the rebels' camp this winter and always praised their actions. They played a significant role in last fall's rebellion. At that time, they stood guard in front of the church and at Trou St Patry.[21] They convinced the *habitants* to follow their example, fearing, so they claimed, that the town's garrison would come to burn their parish.

Ignace Sivadier and Joseph Chabot, the son, gave orders or enlisted *habitants* to stand guard to protect themselves from the attacks that they anticipated would come from the town.

Left for St Pierre at 2:00 P.M.

St Pierre—Ile D'Orléans

Ministered by Monseigr d'Orilé.

Thursday, May 30.

The militia assembled at 5:00 P.M.

The reading of our charges.

Dismissal of:

Frans Leclaire, capt., and Michel Montigny, ensign, for reasons that we will give later.

Discharge of the bailiffs.

Appointment of officers and the reading of their commissions:

Joseph Cauté, Capt.
Prisque Plante, Lieut   May 30
Jean Ferlan, Ensign
Pierre Ferland ⎤
Joseph Gosselin ⎬   Sergeants
Chs Crepau ⎦

Reviewed 120 men.
Public address. [Cheered] "Long live the King" & c.

COMMENTS

François Leclaire, appointed captain last fall, was cashiered and his commission revoked for having carried out the rebels' orders in that rank.

Michel Montigny, ensign, the same for having been a great partisan and zealous supporter of the rebels. It was he who corrupted Capt. Leclaire, encouraged the *habitants* to sedition, prevented them from following all the advice given by Monsignor d'Orilé, and frequently visited the rebels' camp. He was too old to stand guard.

François Chabot and Pierre Choret, the father, sergt. for the rebels, are the two parish spokesmen who opposed Messrs [Adam] Mabane, [William] Grant, and [Nicolas] Boisseau when they wanted to appoint officers last fall.[22]

All winter they went to where the guard stood at the end of the island to encourage the young men in the spirit of rebellion. They did not stand guard because of their old age.

Joseph Langlois [Langlais], "Crooked Neck," and Gabriel Langlais found the parish officers named by Mrs Mabane, Grant, and Boisseau in Mr Desgly's rectory. They assembled the parish at the door. The two men helped the parishioners remove the officers to ensure that they [the people] would not have to carry out orders these men might issue.

Also present were the said Pierre Choret, the son, Jean Goulet, Baptiste Nolin (deceased) and a few others that Monseigr d'Orilé's authority stopped.

Most of the parishioners did not want to get involved in this incident and left without saying anything.

Pierre Naulin, the son, Louis Grégoire, the son, and André Goulet enlisted in the rebel army for 4 months at 40 # per month, but did not receive this pay. Each one only received a pair of cowhide shoes.

The said Joseph Petrus Langlais, "Crooked Neck," kept visiting the rebels' camp during the winter to lodge complaints against several people, especially Monseigr d'Orilé. He did everything he could to prove his zeal for the rebels and to make trouble for loyal subjects. He and his cousin, Gabriel Langlais, were the instigators of having Joseph Cauté, presently capt., taken to the rebels' camp where he was held for ten days. These two are the most dangerous men in this parish; one is 28 years old and the other 30. They have not stood guard often, being more useful to the rebels in other ways.

Louis Ferlan, Louis Dorval, the son, Charles Poulet, François Montigny, Joseph Paradis, the son, and Chatigny constantly went to the rebels' camp last winter and always showed their support of the rebels by their actions.

About a fourth of this parish stood guard willingly for the rebels, some were forced to do so, and the others did not stand guard at all.

Augustin Chabot's wife, ironically nicknamed "The Queen of Hungary" by the *habitants*, perverted almost all the people by spreading her seditious remarks as she went door to door. It seems that this woman has a sharp tongue and, according to the report of several *habitants*, made a strong impression on them with her subversive spirit.

Isaac Goudrau, an Acadian, has been to the rebels' camp very often this winter. He would accompany the *Bostonnais* to act as their interpreter to requisition provisions from Monsr Boisseau's farm and wheat from the Monsr Dupré's mill and other places.[23]

Marin Gourdau doubtful [loyalty].

Brun Gourdau and the widower Gourdau seem to have remained loyal.

Jean Richard Parent, Monsr Boisseau's farmer, proved by his actions that he always remained a good and loyal subject.

Beaulieu from St Roch, who went to Ile d'Orléans last winter, had a certain Govrau from Quebec arrested. He wintered on the said island, saying that he was gathering supplies for the town. He behaved as a disloyal subject all winter.

Nolet Louis Leclaire, the son of a *Bostonnais* capt., Jean Leclaire, and Louis Aubin noted as disloyal subjects.

A certain Joseph Turgeon, a short, blonde-haired man living at Pointe Lévy, took it upon himself to search the countryside for royalists all winter with a *Bostonnais* guard. He intended to take those that he found to the [rebels'] camp as prisoners.

Slept at St Pierre and left the next day at 5:00 A.M. for Quebec.

Left Quebec on Sunday, June 2 at 2:00 P.M. for Ste Foye.

Ste Foye

Ministered by Mr [Ignace] Desroches, Lorette's parish priest.

Sunday, June 2.

The militia assembled at 3:00 P.M.

The reading of our charges.

Dismissal of Capt. Frans Traversy, commissioned by Mr [James] Murray, for having carried out the rebels' orders in that rank and having refused a new commission last fall.

Discharge of the bailiffs.

Appointment of officers acknowledged by the reading of their commissions.

Antoine Samson, Capt.,   commissioned by General Carleton, July 7, 1775.
François Noizeu, Assistant Capt. for Cas [Cap] Rouge, June 2, 1776.[24]
Joseph Migneron, Sergt for Ste Foye.
Michel Masse, Sergt for Cas Rouge.

Public address. [Cheered] "Long live the King" & c.
Reviewed 47 men.

COMMENTS

The named Coska Hamel invited the young men of this parish to take up arms for the rebels the day following the December 31 action.

Dismissal of Guillaume Larose, assistant capt. for the King, for having served the rebels in that rank. Sickness prevented him from attending the review. He did not have a commission.

Louis Routier and Augustin Petitclair have always spoken in favor of the rebels and against the King's interests.

This parish built 225 fascines.[25] Some carried firewood and ladders and performed corvées, most against their will.

The two rebel sergeants were Prisque Lapointe and the above-mentioned Coska Hamel.

Left for St Augustin at 5:00 P.M.

St Augustin

Paris priest, Mr [Louis-Michel] Beriau.

Monday, June 3.

The militia assembled at 9:00 A.M.

The reading of our charges.

Reviewed 150 men.

Shaming of the *habitants* for having assisted the rebels with corvées and various supplies.

Announcement to the *habitants* that for reasons we knew but did not deem necessary to disclose, we would not make public the militia officers [appointed] for this parish; that all past orders would remain valid until new ones arrived.

The bailiffs were reinstated and, therefore, we have given notice [of this] to the hble Lieutenant Gouvr by a letter that we have written to him this day.

Augustin Gingras, appointed capt. by His Excellency General Murray's commission and reconfirmed in his post by His Excellency General Carleton's proclamation, assisted the rebels in this rank with the punctual execution of their orders without any opposition on his part. The same, last fall, refused to accept a new captain's commission. However, he does not seem to have pressured the *habitants* to execute the rebels' orders with his advice or threats. He still is in possession of the commission from General Murray. He did not appoint any junior officers or sergeants this winter on behalf of the rebels, taking care of all their orders himself.

Frans Cauté, known as the capt. of the village of St Augustin although [he had] no commission, carried out the rebels' orders in this rank with much zeal and willingness. We identified him as a disloyal subject. It does not seem that he received a commission from the rebels. No one in the parish took up arms, but it seems that they all performed corvées and provided supplies to the rebels without opposition. It is for this reason that we, despite our information, have been unable to identify loyal subjects. We postponed the appointment of parish officers until another time and cheered, "Long live the King" three times.

Left at 2:00 P.M. for Pointe aux Trembles.

Pointe aux Trembles

Parish priest, Mr [Louis-Eustache Chartier] de Lobinière [Lotbinière].[26]

Tuesday, June 4.

The militia assembled at 9:00 A.M.

The reading of our charges.

Appointed the officers by the reading of their commissions:

Jacques Garnau, Capt.	Appointed by Genl Carln on July 7, 1775.
Louis Gingras, Lieut	June 4.
Frans Belan ⎫	
Joseph Tapin ⎪	
Pierre Ange ⎬	Sergeants
Jean Dussault ⎭	

We formed only one company in this parish, which in the past had been divided into two.

Public address. [Cheered] "Long live the King" & c.

Discharge of the bailiffs.

Reviewed 106 men.

Recommended firmness to the officers when having the King's orders executed.

COMMENTS

Maurice Desdevens, capt. for the rebels, served them with as much zeal as affection.[27] He chose 4 sergeants whom we will name later. He used every effort to have several loyalists looted in this parish; several [loyalists] have been imprisoned on the *Gaspé* upon his recommendation.[28] He tried to incite all the *habitants* to take up arms for the rebels, especially after the December 31 action, saying that the *Bostonnais* were in possession of the Bishop's palace and the powder magazine; that there was no question that a final assault would take the town. He is the reason that several others from this parish sided with the rebels. He fled with them and wrote a letter to Frans Hardy dated the 24 of last month from St Ours, Chambly River, which we have intercepted.[29]

Pignant, a cobbler and roadmender, had the rebels seize about eighteen hundred francs worth of rum belonging to Mr Tonancour [Tonnancour].[30] This rum was brought to le sieur Papillon's house. He praised the rebel forces in this province, and it is noted that he always tried to make trouble for those whom he suspected of loyalty to the King.

Joseph and Jean Goulet's wives went door to door to defame those who, last fall, talked the young men into marching with Mr [Allan] Maclean.[31] They were saying that they would be slaughtered and that if Garnau had not accepted his captain's commission, they would not have to obey such orders.

Those named below were Desdevens' sergeants and have commanded in this rank willingly and enthusiastically, particularly Joseph Martin who issued orders in an arrogant manner, especially towards those whom he believed were royalists.

Romain Dubuc frequently spoke in favor of the rebels, boasting of their strength and belittling that of the town.

Ignace Créqui and Pierre Savary did not show as much enthusiasm for the rebels.

The named Augustin Vezina is believed to have attempted to prevent the nomination of officers for the King last fall.

All the *habitants* of this parish have helped the rebels with transportation.

Left at 1:00 P.M. for Ecureuils.

Ecureuils

Ministered by Mr [Louis-Eustache Chartier] de Lobinière [Lotbinière].

Tuesday, June 4.

The militia assembled at 5:00 P.M.

The reading of our charges.

Discharge of the bailiffs.

Appointment of the officers and the reading of their commissions:

Jacques Delisle, Capt.
Etienne Germain ⎫
François Trépanié ⎬ Sergeants

Public address and an invitation [to the people] to carry their goods to town & c.

Reviewed 36 men. [Cheered] "Long live the King" & c.

COMMENTS

The named Pierre Langlois, a roadmender, was capt. for the rebels.[32] He threatened to ransack [the property of] those who would not acknowledge it. He forced Jean Richard to be his sergeant by threatening to send him to Montreal if he refused.

Nine or ten persons were disarmed on the complaints that he brought against them. In short, he showed as much zeal and affection for the rebels as he did ill will and insolence for the King's service. He went with the rebels and left his wife in this parish.

Left at 6:00 P.M. for Cap Santé.

Cap Santé

Parish priest, Mr [Joseph] Filion [Fillion].

Wednesday, June 5.

The militia assembled at 9:00 A.M.

The reading of our charges.

Discharge of the bailiffs.

Dismissal of Jos. Etienne Pagé, commissioned as a capt. by General Carleton, last July 7, for having served the rebels in his rank of capt. all winter.

Dismissal of the below-named sergeants for the rebels:

Mathurin Mauricet
Augustin Delisle
Jean Pichet
Joseph Louis Pagé
Pierre Girou

They said that they had been forced to accept their position.

Nomination of officers:

Pierre Mercure, Capt.
Pierre Lapare, Lieut
Jean Frans Pagé, Ensign
Antoine Colet
Augustin Richard
Joseph Bertran
Augustin Langlais
Joseph Chalié

Sergeants

Invitation to go to town.

Public address to recommend equity and firmness to the officers when executing the King's orders & c.

Recommendation for the maintenance of the roads.

Reviewed 134 men. [Cheered] "Long live the King" & c.

COMMENTS

The former Capt. Pagé told Pierre Girou that he was making him his sergeant because he absolutely needed one. "You are a poor man and they [the rebels] will pay you forty-eight francs per month." The said Pagé ensured that orders were carried out with diligence and authority.

Frans Germain is said to have held seditious meetings and praised the rebels as early as last fall.

The above-mentioned Pagé, upon the rebels' orders and in his rank of capt., tried to enlist people to bear arms after the incident of [December] 31, but to no avail. He also apparently posted orders forcing the *habitants* to surrender their arms. It is generally believed that this man accepted this commission only because of fear. It is certain that last fall he went with Lieut Col. M'Lean [Maclean] to Sorel and fulfilled his duty very well.

Joseph Mate, Louis Nicolas Mate, and a certain Pagé du Bois from l'Aille refused to perform corvées for the rebels. On the declaration of a capt. who had been asked why three carts were missing, these men were condemned to pay a fine of one écu each to the riflemen.[33] [The riflemen] were sent [to the men's] houses to get them to bring their carts.

The *habitants* of this parish did not take up arms, except for those mentioned above. It seems that they have executed all the orders that they were given without the least resistance on their part. They willingly delivered provisions to the rebels' camp as long as they were paid in money.

Capt. Pagé kept commanding his uncle, Pierre Mercure, despite the latter's objection that he had been exempted from any service by His Excellency General Carleton last fall.

Left for Dechambau [Deschambault] at 2:00 P.M.

Deschambau [Deschambault]

Ministered by Mr [Joseph] Filion [Fillion].

Thursday, June 6.

The militia assembled at 9:00 A.M.

The reading of our charges.

We have discharged Nicolas Pasquin, capt., Pierre Joseph Arcan, lieut, and Joseph Gautier, ensign, for having served the rebels in their respective rank as officers. The first had been commissioned by the King last summer and had appointed the other two as his assistants. N.B. Pierre Jos. Arcan and Joseph Gautier [previously] had served the King in the rank of sergeant.

In the month of February, the following were chosen as officers for the rebels by parish elections.

Philip Baronet *dit* Sans Chagrin, capt. This one appointed the following as subordinates:

Jean Pasquin, his direct assistant
Joseph Marcot, who resides near the church, Major
Joseph Marcot de la Chevrotiere ⎫
Jean Bte Montanbau ⎪
Alexis Letournau ⎬ Sergeants
Jacques Perau ⎪
Antoine Meran ⎭

Discharge of the bailiffs.
Appointment of officers:

Pierre Grolau, Capt.
Joseph Not, Lieut
Jos. Marie Pasquin ⎫
Frans Marcot at Grolau's house ⎪
Mich. Jos. Not ⎬ Sergeants
Augustin Belile ⎭

Public humiliation of the officers named for the rebels this winter and reproach to the parish for that assembly, which was held by a formal order from the rebels, which we have revoked.

Ordered Capt. Pierre Grolau to maintain the greatest discipline among the militia when executing the King's orders.

Public address, & c.

Invitation [to the people] to carry their goods to the town.

Recommendation for the maintenance of the roads.

Reviewed 72 men. [Cheered] "Long live the King."

COMMENTS

Philipe Baronet *dit* San[s] Chagrin
Paul Perrault
Augustin Delisle
Jean Grégoire
St Ours Maillou

Last October, Jean Perrault and several others twice sent a petition to the rebels at St Jean[s] asking for their help.[34]

The messenger was the named Augustin Petit, a farmer for Jean Petizo.

We have ordered le sieur Baronet *dit* Sans Chagrin to produce the commission that he had received from the rebels in order to burn it publicly. He answered that he had [already] surrendered it to Capt. Little John [Littlejohn].[35]

During the rebels' retreat, the young boys, Paul and Jean Perrault, guided Maurice Desdevens to St Ours on the Chambly River in return for a cow that he gave them. They said that they did not know that he was a well-known rebel.

Joson Péron publicly enlisted the *habitants* to furnish provisions to the rebels during their retreat, saying that "if everyone was like me, they would not have to leave."

The *habitants* of this parish have assisted the rebels with transportation during the winter, and it seems that most did so willingly. Similarly, they have also taken apart several cannons and carried them to their [the rebels'] entrenchments at Dechambau [Deschambault].[36]

The rebels unearthed and took 3 cannons, which had been left in this area since the last war.

Left for [Les] Grondines at 11:00 A.M.

[Les] Grondines

Ministered by Mr [Louis-Michel] Guay.

Thursday, June 6.

The militia assembled at 5:00 P.M.

The reading of our charges.

Meeting where we called, in particular, the bailiffs, their assistants, and the militia officers that we have questioned on the conduct of the parish.

Consulted with the priest to the choice of officers to appoint.

Dismissal of the following:

Louis Trotier, Capt.

Frans Boivert

Bernard Trotier   } Sergeants

Nicolas Rivard

Discharge of the bailiffs.

Appointment of new officers acknowledged by the reading of their commissions:

Joseph Amelin *dit* Paynol, Capt.

René Trotier Houssard

René Trotier   } Sergeants

Charles Lecuyer

Reviewed 37 men.

Public address. [Cheered] "Long live the King" & c.

COMMENTS

Louis Trotier, capt., commissioned by General Murray, March 3, 1764, and by General Carleton on July 7, 1775, served the rebels in this rank, if not with zeal, at least with vigilance, believing that it was his duty. He threatened Jean Bte Sauvageau with being taken to the rebels' camp under guard, if he did not obey their orders. His subordinates were:

Chs Boivert, Lieut   } both dead
Frans Trotier, Ensign

Frans Boivert
Bernard Trotier   } have served in the role of sergeant for the rebels.
Nicolas Rivard

This parish carried out all corvées without resistance, but it does not seem that the spirit of rebellion reigns.

Left for Ste Anne at 7:00 P.M.

Ste Anne

Parish priest, Mr [Louis-Michel] Guay.

Friday, June 7.

The militia assembled at 9:00 A.M.
The reading of our charges.
Called forth:

Louis Goin [Gouin], Capt. for the King[37]
Nicolas Dury, Lieut   do
Jacques Montreuil, Ensign do
Joachim Chatelrau
Batiste Barré   } Sergeants do
[no name] Morel

After having reproached them for having served the rebels in <u>their</u> roles as officers, we have discharged them, except for Louis Goin [Gouin], for reasons we that will give below.

Called forth:

Joseph Lanouet, Capt. for the rebels since March
Pierre Baribau, Lieut do

Pierre Pigué, Ensign, and the sergeants mentioned above.

We asked them if they had accepted commissions. They answered no. They had been chosen by parish elections ordered by the rebel commander of 3 Rivières.[38] We declared them unworthy of ever holding any government position.

Discharge of the bailiffs.

Appointed as officers:

Louis Goin [Gouin], Capt., commissioned by Genl. Carleton,
    June 22, 1775.
Joachim Lanouet, Lieut
Paul Frigon, Ensign
Joseph Lanouet, the son ⎫
Antoine Charest, the son ⎪
Michel Baribau   ⎬ Sergeants
Bte Nobert   ⎪
Alexis Vallé   ⎭

We have severely reproached Louis Goin [Gouin] for having served the rebels in the rank of capt. We publicly declared that we would have dismissed him if several of his courageous deeds in support of the government had not been brought to our attention.

The entire parish knew of his great zeal in executing the King's orders last fall, which attracted the indignation of a great number in this parish. He was pillaged, disarmed and insulted on several occasions. Last fall he led a party of 22 young men from this parish to Montreal to fight the rebels. In short, he always protected those of this parish who were loyal to the King.

Recommended to the officers to keep the roads in good condition and to execute the King's orders with very great diligence.

Public address and invitation to carry their goods to Quebec.

Reviewed 104 men.

[Cheered] "Long live the King" & c.

COMMENTS

Joseph Lanouet went with two *Bostonnais* riflemen to force the widow Goin's [Gouin] daughters to provide a cart to the rebels.

Campanais, who lives in bonhomme Nicolas's house, said to Goin [Gouin] one day as they left the church, "you are no longer under the English government. You must now answer to the *Bostonnais.*" Last fall he opposed the King's orders. He tried to incite the *habitants* to take up arms for the rebels and often publicly boasted of their strength. In short, he is the one who is the most responsible for corrupting this parish.

Last fall, Rampené, Baptiste le Duc, and Devau tried to deter the young men from the parish who had received orders to go to Montreal. They suggested that the *habitants* present a petition to the rebels to force Louis Goin [Gouin] to return the money that they had paid as a fine upon Colonel McLean's [Maclean] orders.

This parish helped the rebels with transportation without resistance, and some delivered provisions to their camp.

Left for Batiscant [Batiscan] at 2:00 P.M.

Batiscant [Batiscan]

Ministered by Mr [Charles-Joseph] Lefevre [Lefebvre-Duchouquet].[39]

Friday, June 7.

The militia assembled at 5:00 P.M.

The reading of our charges.

Called forth:

Alexis Marchand, Capt. for the King, Absent.
Pierre Frigon, Lieut,   do

We have discharged them for reasons that we will give below.
Called forth:

Alexis Marchand, Capt. for the rebels.
Claude Carignant, Lieut   do
Pierre Sainsire, Ense   do
Jean Trotier   }
                        Sergts do
Joseph Suval   }

Les sieurs Alexis Marchand and Pierre Sainsire [Frigon?] being absent, we asked le sieur <u>Claude</u> Carignan[t] if they had received commissions from the *Bostonnais*, which he denied. After having impressed upon them the seriousness of their error, we have declared them unworthy of ever holding any government position.

Discharge of the bailiffs.

Appointment of the officers:

Jean Trotier, the father, Capt.
Antoine Lanouet, Lieut
Joseph Carignant   }
                      Sergeants
Baptiste Lizé   }

Public address to the officers to recommend firmness and diligence when executing the King's orders, to maintain the roads, and to encourage the people to carry their goods and food to Quebec & c.

Reviewed 18 men. [Cheered] "Long live the King" & c.

COMMENTS

Le sieur Alexis Marchand served the rebels as a capt. with zeal and affection. He had shown much reluctance in accepting the commission of the King last fall. He chose his own sergeants after having been made capt. for the rebels by parish election, as were the officers named above. He sent Pierre Sainsire, his ensign, to tell Pierre Frigon that if he did not surrender the lieut's commission that he received from the King last fall, he would send four riflemen to take him by force to face the *Bostonnais* commander of Trois Rivières.

It seems that Pierre Frigon was dismissed by the parish this winter because he had the King's orders executed with great resolve. Although he served the rebels as an officer, his feelings have always remained in favor of the King's party.

This parish provided transportation for the rebels without any resistance. Left for Ste Geneviève at 1:00 P.M., Saturday, June 8.

Rivière Batiscant [Batiscan], Ste Geneviève

Ministered by Mr [Charles-Joseph] Lefevre [Lefebvre-Duchouquet].

Saturday, June 8.

The militia assembled at 3:00 P.M.
The reading of our charges.
Dismissal of Antoine Lacourcière, Capt.

Baptiste Chatauneuf, Lieut
François Trudel, Ensign
Joseph Lafontaine ⎫
Antoine Porvénau ⎭ Sergeants

Discharge of the bailiffs.
Appointment of the officers acknowledged by the reading of their commissions:

Joseph Belletête, Capt.
Jean Trépanier, Lieut   Commissioned June 8.

Louis Lheureux
Louis Guidau Lefevre ⎫
Joseph Saternau ⎬ Sergeants
Baptiste Cosset ⎭

Reviewed 64 men.
Public address. [Cheered] "Long live the King" & c.

COMMENTS

The officers and sergts named above were cashiered. Although they had received commissions from General Carleton last fall, they executed the rebels' orders in their roles during the course of the winter until their escape. They used the same threats in their orders that the rebels used on them in case they did not obey.

The said Capt. Lacoursière [Lacourcière], in obedience to the rebels' orders, surrendered his commission to the alleged commander of Trois Rivières. In executing his orders, he [Lacourcière] held an assembly of the whole parish at his house to elect new militia officers, which maintained all of them in their respective rank.

This parish seems to have very willingly obeyed all orders, mainly to provide carts for the rebels.

The new capt. and lieut did not attend the assembly because they were not informed of it. We have sent them their commissions and wrote them a letter in which we urged them to execute the King's orders with all possible diligence; to send us in Quebec their company roll within a few days; to withdraw Ba[p]tiste Chatauneuf's commission as militia lieutenant and include this with the said roll.

Left for Champlain at 6:00 P.M.

Champlain

Ministered by Mr [Charles-Joseph] Lefevre [Lefebvre-Duchouquet].

Sunday, June 9.

The militia assembled at 8:00 A.M.

The reading of our charges.

Dismissal of:

Chorel Dorvilier, Capt.,   commissioned by General
Jean Grammont, Lieut   Carleton last fall

Discharge of the bailiffs.

Appointment of the officers acknowledged by the reading of their commissions:

Jean Jacqs Leblanc, Capt.

Joseph Chartier, Lieut

Josh Rau *dit* Alexandre

Alexis Bodouin   Sergeants

Reviewed 30 men.

Public address. [Cheered] "Long live the King" & c.

COMMENTS

The above-mentioned Capt. Dorvilier seems to have always kept the sentiments of a loyal subject. However, he served as a capt. for the rebels this winter because of his commission from General Carleton. He surrendered it to the rebels this winter in obedience to their orders.

He seems to have done so because of fear and weakness.

Jean Grammont, Lieutenant, the same.

Grovil Beaudouin was named ensign by the parish election when it reappointed the other two officers.

Jean Chartier has served in the role of sergeant for the rebels since April.

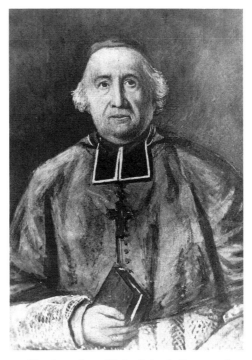

*Monsignor Jean-Olivier Briand. Courtesy of
the National Archives of Canada (C-6876).*

The so-called Beaudouin, the <u>said</u> parish's butcher, seems to have always given bad advice. Last fall, he spoke irreverently to Mr de Lanaudière, the son, complaining about a dispute that he had concerning some rectory matters with several of its residents.[40] The *habitants* advised him to consult the Grand Vicar [Etienne Montgolfier] or Monsignor, the Bishop [Jean-Olivier Briand] [concerning the problem] whenever they could be approached.[41] Beaudouin retorted that he did not acknowledge the Bishop's authority nor that of the Grand Vicar and that he would take his complaints to the *Bostonnais* commander at Trois Rivières.

This parish obeyed the rebels' orders without resistance.

Left at 1:00 P.M. for Cap [La] Madelaine.

Cap La Madelaine

Ministered by Mr [Pierre Garreau *dit* Saint-Onge] Saintonge, Vicar General of Trois Rivières.[42]

Sunday, June 9.

The militia assembled at 4:00 P.M.
The reading of our charges.
Dismissal of:

Jean Bte Lacroix, Capt.
Crevier Belrive, Lieut
Jacques Lacroix, Ensign

Discharge of the bailiffs.
Nomination of officers acknowledged by the reading of their commissions:

Joseph Lacroix, Capt.
Antoine Belony, Lieut
Isidore Lacroix
[no name] Toupin, the son   } Sergeants

Reviewed 26 men.
Public address. [Cheered] "Long live the King" & c.

COMMENTS

Jean Bte Lacroix, Crevier Belrive, and Jacques Lacroix had received commissions last summer from His Excellency General Carleton. This winter, each in their respective rank, carried out the rebels' orders without any resistance on their part.

Joseph Vivier served in the role of sergeant. This winter, the rebels gave orders to the officers commissioned by General Carleton to remit their commissions and to call parish elections to name new officers. As a result, all the *habitants* assembled at the above-named Capt. Jean Bte Lacroix's house. They unanimously reappointed the same officers and sergeant, who seem to have eagerly executed all the rebels' orders, especially the said capt. [Lacroix].

Dorval, the father of Michel Dorval, the bailiff, seems to have always made disparaging remarks against the King's party. He even implied that the Bishop of Quebec and the Vicar General of Trois Rivières had been paid to preach submission to the King.

Joseph Bomier also was noted for being a strong partisan of the rebels.

This parish did not take up arms but performed corvées [for the rebels] without resistance.

Crossed to Trois Rivières at 6:00 P.M.

To Trois Rivières

Sunday evening, June 9, detained by order of His Excellency General Carleton to await new orders.

Thursday, June 13, ordered to cross to Bécancour tomorrow in order to continue our mission.

Friday [June] 14, crossed to Bécancour at 11:00 A.M.

Bécancour

Missionary priest, Father Théodore [Loiseau].

Saturday, June 15.

The militia assembled at 8:00 A.M.
The reading of our charges.
Dismissal of:

Joseph Feuilletau, Capt.
Antoine Desilet, Lieut   Company Officers of Fleuve
Frans Tourigny, Ensign   and Rivière Bécancour[43]
Chs Provanché ⎫
Laurent Tourigny ⎭   Serg.

Same

Pierre Cormier *dit* Perot, Capt.	Company Officers
Frans Bourque, Lieut	of Lac St Paul
Michel Bergeront, Ensign	established by the
Thimothé Leprince, Sergeant	Acadians[44]

Discharge of the bailiffs.

Appointment of new officers acknowledged by the reading of their commissions:

Alixis Leblanc, Capt. Commissioned on June 14, first company including Fleuve and Rivière Bécancour

Joseph Bourgeois, Lieut (commissioned on June 15)

Bonaventure Bauchêne
Jacques Richard ⎫ Sergts
Jean Doucet ⎭

Benony Bourque, Capt. Second company including Lac St Paul established by the Acadians (commissioned on June 15)

Etienne Hébert ⎫ Sergts
Pierre Prince ⎭

Reviewed sixty-eight men of the first company and 5 men representing the second company because not all could come, being occupied with making boats for the King's service.

After gathering and verifying our information, we have called forth in the presence of the entire parish:

Joseph Levasseur
Chs Provanché
Larant Tourigny
Pierre Cormier *dit* Perot

François Bourque
Michel Bergeront

We demanded the commissions that each had received in their respective roles as militia officers following the election that a parish assembly held in obedience to the rebels' orders. They surrendered these commissions, except for the last two officers named above, who did not bring them. Having a torch brought to us, we condemned the six alleged officers named above. [We made] each of them hold the said commission in one hand and burn it with the other in the absence of an executioner, which was done immediately.

COMMENTS

Joseph Feuilletau, Antoine Desilet, and François Tourigny, had been commissioned by General Carleton last summer, and had served the rebels in their roles as officers until they organized the election of new ones. It seems that they only acted out of weakness rather than affection for the rebels.

Chs Provanché and Laurent Tourigny served in the role of sergeant.

In February, the parish assembled to appoint militia officers and chose for the first company:

Joseph Levasseur, Capt.
Chs Provanché, Lieut
Laurent Tourigny, Ense
Alexis Tourigny ⎤
Guenoche Desilet ⎬ Sergts
Jean Darouin ⎦

N.B. The alleged Capt. Levasseur seems to be a dangerous subject, who carried out his orders with threats, vigilance, zeal, and willingness.

The officers of the second company in Lac St Paul were reappointed and have acted as such without the least resistance. Following the said election, the rebels forced the officers appointed by General Carleton to turn in their commissions and later sent the alleged officers the commissions that we had them burn. However, as the said François Bourque and Michel Bergeront had not brought theirs, we have ordered Capt. Benony Bourque to get them [the commissions] and attach them with his company's roll, which he is ordered to send us within a few days.

This parish performed corvées [for the rebels] but did not take up arms, except for a young boy, Simon Marchand, and de Saint Pierre, a married man, who enlisted to bear arms for the pay of 40 # per month. They have been home since the month of May.

The rebels forced Chs Massé to carry a load [of supplies] to their camp for having refused the alleged Capt. Levasseur's orders to go with the others [parishioners] to Champlain or Batiscant [Batiscan].

The same [Levasseur] lodged a complaint against Joseph Levasseur from Rapide for the same reason.

[Levasseur] for the same reason against Jean Gagnon of the Lac St Paul company of Acadians.

When a complaint was lodged against someone who refused to obey orders, the rebels would send riflemen to force-march those who resisted.

Left for Gentilly at 1:00 P.M.

Gentilly

Ministered by Father Théodore [Loiseau].

Saturday, June 15.

The militia assembled at 4:00 P.M.

The reading of our charges.

This parish would not receive officers last fall.

[Results of the] parish elections held last February by order of the rebels:

Chs Chandonet, Capt.

Louis Normandin, Lieut

Joseph Courville, Ensign

Joseph Turigni ⎫
Joseph Giroire ⎭ Sergeants

Called forth the above-mentioned and asked them if they had received commissions from the rebels, and they answered no. After having shamed them for their disgraceful conduct, we have declared them unfit of ever holding any government position.

Discharge of the bailiffs.

We have appointed as officers:

Antoine Poisson, Capt.
Daniel Labissonière, Lieut
Alexis Poisson ⎱
Antoine Rivard ⎰ Sergeants

We have recommended that the officers maintain discipline and vigilance when executing the King's orders and that they show great care in keeping the roads in good repair.

Invited the *habitants* to carry their goods and other items to town & c.

Reviewed 31 men. [Cheered] "Long live the King" & c.

COMMENTS

The two young brothers, Michel Laroche and Jean Laroche, have served the rebels at their Quebec encampment from All Saints Day [November 1] until last May for 40 # per month.[45]

They are presently residing in this parish where they own a plot of land.

Baptiste Carignant, the son of Frans Carignant, enrolled, as did the above-mentioned individuals, in the company of a certain [Ethan?] Allen; he [Carignant] is presently living at his father's house.[46]

Last fall, Chs Chandonnet [Chandonet], a capt. for the rebels, refused a commission from the King, and the whole parish seems to have resisted receiving them.

This winter, the rebels only once required these parishioners to carry 14 carts of supplies to their camp in front of Quebec.

Left for St Pierre at 7:00 P.M.

St Pierre de le'bequest
[St Pierre des Becquets]

Missionary priest, Father Louis, Rector.

Sunday, June 16.

The militia assembled at 8:00 A.M.

The reading of our charges.

Called forth and discharged for the reasons that we will give below:

Pierre Viola, Capt.

Guillaume Bertrand, Lieut   commissioned for

Antoine Trotier, Ense   the King last fall

We declared them unworthy of ever holding any government position.

Officers appointed by parish elections last February upon the rebels' orders:

Augustin Brisson, Capt.

Joseph Maillot, Lieut

Augustin Trotier, Ense

Baptiste Lafond ⎤

Louis Grondin   ⎬   Sergeant

Bte Touzignant ⎦

Called [them] forth and asked if they had received commissions from the rebels, and they answered no. After shaming them for their scandalous behavior, we declared them unfit to ever hold any government position.

Discharge of the bailiffs.

We have appointed as officers:

Pierre Roberge, Capt.

Jean Moras, Lieut

Chas Barry   ⎤

Alexis Brouillet ⎦   Sergeants

We have recommended that they maintain obedience and vigilance when executing the King's orders and keeping the roads in good repair.

Reviewed 36 men. [Cheered] "Long live the King" & c.

COMMENTS

Pierre Viola posted an order from the rebels on the church doors, which forbade the parish from communicating with the town. In February, he turned in the commissn that he had received last fall for the King to the rebel commander of Trois Rivières. He does not appear, however, to have served willingly and, before these usurpers had occupied the province, he had served the King with zeal.

He spoke favorably of the royalists several times during the winter.

Le sieur Guillaume Bertrand remitted [to the rebels] the commission that he had received for the King without the least resistance. This is the reason for which he was dismissed.

Last fall, le sieur Antoine Trotier refused to accept his commission as ensign for the King. It [the commission] always remained in the capt.'s possession. This was the reason for which he was not reappointed.

A certain number of *habitants* from this parish presented the commander of the Congress's army with a petition, which we have copied. [The petition] was against those who disapproved of their zeal for the rebels and against their pastor for refusing them the sacraments.

This complaint brought a reprimand and threats to Father Louis, their parish priest, from the rebel commander's aide-de-camp in a December 30 letter, which we have revoked.[47]

Last fall, nine *habitants* of this parish under the leadership of a certain Brisset from Chambly, self-proclaimed capt. for the rebels' service, went to the house of the said Louis Goin [Gouin] from Ste Anne. They insulted him several times and threatened to burn his house. They forced him to give them 96 shillings of this province in cash, a few supplies, and some weapons. These scoundrels claimed that they had been authorized by Mr [Richard] Montgomery.

We have their names and the details of this affair from a letter that le sieur Louis Goin [Gouin] wrote last March 3 to Father Louis, of which we have a copy.

The *habitants*, who presented the petition which we spoke of above, stood guard for ten days around All Saints Day in the lower section of this parish under the command of the named Chs Brisset to prevent the King's troops from looting or burning their parish.

The rebels twice required that this parish assist them with transporting supplies; some [supplies were transported] to Pointe aux Trembles and others to their camp.

The names of those who have presented the petition and stood guard: Michel Perault, Bazil Perault, Tilly Brisson, Valentin Maillot, Prisque Maillot, Chandonet, Jacques Baptiste Antoine Touzignant, Frans Barry, Antoine Spenard, Gabril Spenard, Frans Grondin, Joseph Maillot, and Alexis Maillot.

Names of those who have insulted or looted Goin [Gouin]:

Frans Barry, Gabriel Spenard, Chandonet, Antoine Spenard, Jacques Langlais, Bte Touzignant, Valentin Maillot, Prisque Maillot, and François Grondin with Chs Brisset.

Left for St Jean at 1:00 P.M.

St Jean de l'Echaillon [Deschaillons]

Ministered by Father Louis.

Sunday, June 16.

The militia assembled at 3:00 P.M.

The reading of our charges.

Dismissal of Nicolas Maillot, Capt.

Discharge of the bailiffs.

Appointment of a captain acknowledged by the reading of his commission:

Jacques Bodet, Capt.

Joseph Laliberté ⎫
Bazil Charland ⎭   Sergeants

Reviewed 22 men.

Public address. [Cheered] "Long live the King" & c.

This parish did not receive any orders from the government last summer. When Mr L['E]cuyer made his journey through the countryside in the Quebec district to appoint militia officers, he gave a capt.'s commission to Nicolas Maillot, first bailiff of this parish.[48] The said Maillot neglected, or rather, lacked the resolve to serve as captain of the parish and always acted as a bailiff. We have dismissed him for this reason.

The rebels did not send any orders to this parish during the entire time that they occupied this province. They did not appoint officers this winter, as they did in the other parishes.

Valentin Maillot and Baptiste Touzignant voluntarily joined the people from St Pierre. Five or six other *habitants* were swayed by the counsel of the first two and by those from St Pierre to join them and stand guard, but they only stayed for a very short period of time.

Left for Lobinière [Lotbinière] at 5:00 P.M.

Lobinière [Lotbinière]

Parish priest, Mr [Jean-Baptiste] Gauin [Gatien].

Monday, June 17.

The militia assembled at 1:00 P.M.

The reading of our charges.

Called forth and dismissed:

Baptiste Hamel	bailiffs for the King and who
Baptiste Bodet,	served the rebels in that rank.

We have declared them unworthy of ever holding any government position. Appointed as officers:

Jean Leclair, Capt.
Frans Bellanger, Lieut
Louis Lemay
Joseph Fignau
Joseph Lherau
Frans Belanger [Bellanger], the son

Sergeants

Public address as usual.
Reviewed 53 men. [Cheered] "Long live the King" & c.

COMMENTS

The said Ignace Lemay refused the commission of capt. for the King last fall. Almost all the parish was in agreement at this time not to accept officers. They said that they preferred having the bailiffs because since they [bailiffs] were reappointed each year they would not commit injustices. This was not so with a captain, who had a fixed term.

Joseph and Michel Bodet went to the rebels' camp twice to deliver provisions.

Last fall, a good number [of people] proposed to stand guard to oppose any incursion that they suspected the King's troops would make, but this project was not executed.

The rebels requested only two corvées from this parish, which consisted of supplying them with about 30 carts, some for Pointe aux Trembles and the rest for their camp in front of Quebec.

Left for Ste Croix at 3:00 P.M.

Ste Croix

Ministered by Mr [Jean-Baptiste] Noël.

Tuesday, June 18.

The militia gathered at 8:00 A.M.
The reading of our charges.
Dismissal of Joseph Duquet, Capt.

Discharge of the bailiffs.

Appointment of officers acknowledged by the reading of their commissions:

Antoine Hamel, Capt.	as of June 18
Joseph Simon Houle, Lieut	

Joseph Hamel, the son ⎫
Gervais Grenier ⎪
Jean Louis Hamel ⎬ Sergeants
Frans Bergeront ⎭

Reviewed 60 men.

Public address. [Cheered] "Long live the King" & c.

COMMENTS

Firstly, Capt. Joseph was dismissed for having neglected to acknowledge his captaincy when he received his commission last summer; secondly, for having served the rebels in this rank last winter, and for having orders executed by Louis Hamel. [Duquet] had [Hamel] named his sergeant or subordinate officer by the authority of a rebel officer whom he was guiding to the neighboring parish.

The said Louis Hamel declared that he did everything possible to be relieved of all commands. However, in his presence, Jos. Duquet explained to the said *Bostonnais* officer that he could not oversee the whole parish by himself. [Duquet] needed help supervising the upper section [of the parish]. Upon such considerations, the above-mentioned *Bostonnais* officer said to the said Louis Hamel that he had to serve or else he would send him to the general's headquarters. Consequently, since that time, Hamel executed all the rebels' orders under the authority of Capt. Duquet. He has overseen road repairs and provided horses to carry two cannons. He has also supervised several other corvées, helping the rebels with transportation upon the request, or rather, the orders of Capt. Pagé at Cap Santé. According to the statement of many *habitants* from Ste Croix, Pagé forced this parish to perform corvées [for the rebels] and threatened them if they refused.

~~Last October, several *habitants* gathered at Jacques Bergeron's house for four to five days to protect themselves from others who would come to burn their property. They acted that way having heard malicious rumors spreading all along the southern coast that the English were burning the countryside.~~ This note was proven false so we crossed it out.

It does not seem that any of these *habitants* took up arms for the rebels.

Left for St Antoine at noon.

N.B. Since le sieur Joseph Duquet was not home at the time of the review, we have ordered Capt. Hamel to withdraw the commission that he had received last summer from Genl Carleton. He is to attach it to his company roll, which he must send to us by the first day [of the month].

N.B. Last Nbre General Carleton sent a frigate with two other vessels to block the passage of the vessels that Montgomery had seized.[49] When Capt. Pagé from Cap Santé saw our vessels anchored in front of his house, he went to find [Benedict] Arnold at Mercure's house in Pte aux Trembles. He [Pagé] requested troops to stop the vessels' ascent. Arnold gave him 60 men and [gun]powder and [musket]balls for the *habitants*.[50]

[Two pages have been torn from the manuscript. They contained the report for St Antoine and the beginning of one for St Nicolas. The text continues as it is in the original].

Wednesday, June 19.

Bailiffs [were appointed] in the said rank of bailiffs.

This fall the rebels ordered 30 carts from the said parish to transport the flour seized at St Nicolas's mill to Sault de la Chaudière.[51]

This parish also provided horses for transporting cannons and for other various trips.

On March 26, the named Joseph Champagne, a *habitant* from St Joseph at Nouvelle Beauce, entered the said Capt. Louis Jacqs Roussau's house and inquired if he had seen two men.[52] The said capt. replied that he had. "Ah good" replied the said Champagne. "They are the two rascals who are trying to come into the town. You must have them apprehended right away" (the

View of the Falls of the Chaudière, by James Peachey. Courtesy of the National Archives of Canada (C-2004).

said Champagne was coming from Ste Foye and was returning to la Beauce). On this report, the said Capt. Rousseau ordered Joseph Bergeront and Pierre Gingras to arm themselves and help him capture the two men, which they immediately did. They took these two men to Capt. Lambert's house, then the said Joseph Bergeront and Pierre Gingras returned home. However, the said Capt. Rousseau thought it better, or maybe he had received orders, to take these two prisoners to the [rebels'] camp in front of Quebec, where he had received from a certain Benoît [Benedict] Arnold a capt.'s commission dated March 27. He had the boldness to accept a capt. assistant's and a lieutenant's commission in the name of Joseph Loignon and Joseph Demerse, who had never volunteered to receive them. We ordered the said Louis Jacqs Rousseau to remit these commissions to us. After having read them publicly as a mock proclamation in front of the assembled militia, we told him that all sundry papers from the rebels, whether orders or commissions, had to be burned by a public executioner. Because it would take too long to have one come, we were condemning him to act as his own. The sentence was carried out immediately and afterwards we declared him unworthy and unfit of ever holding any government position.

Les sieurs Jean Brum and Joseph Winter were captured this winter at Pierre Gingras's home by a *Bostonnais* guard. They had been directed to Revd Father Bonaventure, the parish priest, who, knowing Joseph Demerse's good feelings for the government, sent them to him.

The said Joseph Demerse kept them at his home until the next day. Fearing that they would be discovered since they had asked for directions on the way [to his house], he spoke to his neighbor, Pierre Gingras, who received and hid them willingly. The first night, the two men lay hidden in the stable and the second inside the house, where they were captured around midnight. The said sieurs Brum and Winter had offered the aforesaid Jos. Demerse and Pierre Gingras four piastres, even eight, to guide them to town. Demerse and Gingras protested that they had not asked for a sou, fearing that if they were arrested [their houses] would be burned and ransacked.[53] But they promised to find some way of getting them there.

Pierre Gingras, thus, convinced his brother to guide them [to town], saying that since he was a young man, he was less likely to arouse suspicion and that he could use his canoe to accompany the two men to Quebec. They intended to follow this plan had they not been caught that night.

It seems that they were discovered for having imprudently asked directions to Joseph Demerse's house from a certain Coutur from Pte Lévy, whom they met on their way. These two men aroused Coutur's suspicion, and he mentioned his encounter to Capt. Lambert at Pte Lévy, who immediately alerted the rebels.

Capt. Lambert from Rivière Très Chemins ordered Joseph Gingras, a *habt* from St Nicolas, to tell Michel Dupon, the bailiff's assistant from the parish, to arrest two royalists. He [Dupon] well knew that these two men were at Jean Bte Dumais's house, as a result of Mr Lambert's orders being carried out by Joseph Gingras. Without further authority, Mr Michel Dupon ordered Joseph Dumais, Frans Douvil, Louis Dumais, Pierre Gingras and the above-mentioned Joseph Gingras to help him go arrest the two men, who were hidden at Jean Bte Louis Dumais's house. Not finding them in the house, they noticed a trail that led to the woods. They followed it and found the two men, whom they immediately seized. The said Jean Bte Louis Dumais, having also been ordered to deliver the two captured men in his cart, convinced Joseph Demerse to accompany him with one of the two arrested men, with the intent of letting his prisoner escape. He proceeded with his cart, but they met the *Bostonnais* guard to whom they surrendered their prisoner.[54]

N.B. Capt. Louis Jacqs Roussau and the bailiff Michel Dupon could not give the names of the 4 Canadians that they had arrested.

Denis Frichet, upon leaving church last summer after having heard a sermon by the parish priest extolling obedience to the King, shouted in front of everyone "What is our priest talking about now? What business is he meddling in, talking like an Englishman?"

It does not seem that any member of this parish enlisted to serve and bear arms for the rebels during the winter.

Left for Quebec at 3:00 P.M.

Left Quebec for St Henry at 1:00 P.M. Monday, June 24.

St Henry

Ministered by Mr [Jean-Jacques] Berthiome [Berthiaume].[55]

Monday, June 24.

The militia assembled at 5:00 P.M.

The reading of our charges.

The government never having appointed officers in this parish, the King's orders have been carried out by the bailiffs.

We have discharged those named below for having carried out the rebels' orders in their rank as bailiff:

François Morin
Louis Bussière
Louis Paradis

Appointed as officers:

Pierre Crespau, Capt.
Louis Begein, Lieut
Jacques Letourneur ⎤
J. Bte Crespau   ⎟
André Godebou   ⎬ Sergeants
Joseph Fontaine   ⎦

Public address. Reviewed 57 men. [Cheered] "Long live the King" & c.

COMMENTS

The three above-mentioned bailiffs have ordered this parish to make ladders, and to carry them and the beams taken from the seigniorial mill to Pointe Lévy. Lastly, they have ordered [the people] to go with the rebels to fight Monsr Beaujeu's party.

The names of those, some armed with rifles and others with sticks, who took part in the action at the said Michel Blay's house:[56]

Bonhomme Laverdure, Ignace Allé, Antoine Nadeau, Pierre Jacques, Joseph Arguin, Paul Arguin, Etienne Paradis, the son, Pierre Jourdoin, the son of Sans Chagrin, and another whose name we have been unable to learn.

They all returned home after 4 days.

A certain [Pierre] Ayot[te] from the lower coast also came here to command this expedition.[57]

The said Baptiste Deschamps and Jérôme Arguin served in the rebels' camp for 40 # per month from November until March. The first received only 6 measures of flour for pay, and the second did not get anything.

This parish built 200 ladders as corvées upon the rebels' assurance of [receiving] two shillings per day. They were also to transport them and the beams that the rebels took from the seigniorial mill to Pointe Lévy.

Last fall, the majority of *habitants* went in small, armed groups to Pointe Lévy where a rather large number of *habitants* from other parishes had also gathered. They had marched at the invitation of a few deputies who were sent to them from Pointe Lévy. Their intention was to strengthen each other's resolve not to take up arms for the government. They also wanted to prevent the enlistment of those from Pointe Lévy who had been forced to do so.

Almost everyone from this parish seems to have aided and assisted the rebels with much zeal.

Left for La Beauce, Tuesday, 25 of this month [June] at 4:00 P.M.

Nouvelle Beauce—Ste Marie Parish

Parish priest, Mr Verrau [Verreau].

Wednesday, June 26.

The militia assembled at 10:00 A.M.

The reading of our charges.

Dismissal of Capt. Etienne <u>Parant</u> and of Lieutenant Julien Landry.

Discharge of the bailiffs.

Appointment of officers acknowledged by the reading of their commissions:

François Verrau, Capt.
Guillaume Provost, Lieut
Philipe Valière ⎤
Benjamin Dion ⎟
Frans Mauricet ⎬ Sergeants
Jean Frans Bisson ⎟
Gabriel Fauché ⎦

Reviewed 115 men.

Public address. [Cheered] "Long live the King" & c.

COMMENTS

In the course of May 1775, Mr [Gabriel] Taschereau came to this parish by order of Genl Carleton to establish the militia and appoint a captain. He did this without meeting any opposition on the part of the *habitants* and appointed le sieur Etienne Parant, the father, capt.

Sometime later, Mr Launière had a government order sent to the said Capt. Parant to arrest three spies who had come down the St John River and were traveling up to La Beauce through the Chaudière River.[58] Consequently, the said Parant, who knew that the three aforesaid spies were at Claude Patry's house, warned them to leave because he had orders to arrest them. During the night, he sent the wife of a certain Provençal, his neighbor, who spoke English [to warn them]. The next morning, he ordered Julien Landry, his lieut, Fabien Routier, Antoine Marcoux, Louis Parant, Ignance Ferland and Charles Huard to the neighboring parish [in pursuit], but they went slowly for fear of catching them. He similarly allowed other unidentified people to pass through the parish several times, against his orders.

When the rebels passed through the said parish last fall, the said Parant gave them proof of his zeal and affection at Claude Patry's home, where a great number of them had gathered.[59] He admitted to them that far from arresting their spies, he had, on the contrary, helped their passage. He had offered them his home and several had even slept in his house. During the winter, he went to Rivière du Sud to buy wheat seeds and spread a rumor that since a *Bostonnais* party was coming down through La Beauce again, it was necessary that he promptly return to supply them.[60]

This man, who at first showed his zeal and affection for the King's service, has been corrupted by his wife, whose spirit always spread discord among the *habitants*. She has made a thousand disparaging remarks about the priests and all honest people from this parish. Notably, during this given episode, she never stopped making seditious remarks to everyone in this parish and in all the neighboring ones.

Last fall, Jacques Parant, son of Capt. Parant, went with Joseph Gagnon to St Joseph parish to meet with the rebels. He said that the *habitants* of Pointe Lévy urged them to come promptly because the King wanted them to take up arms and had already confiscated all their canoes. The said Jacques Parant assured us that he had been no further than Louis Marcoux's house, his father-in-law, where he found two *Bostonnais*, to whom he disclosed the intentions of Pointe Lévy's *habitants*. The two *Bostonnais* immediately left with the said Jacques Parant for Claude Patry's house. One of the *Bostonnais* took the said Patry's horse to alert his army of the plans of *habitants* in Pointe Lévy.

The named Jacq. Ducharme and Gervais Houle carried this alleged "invitation" from the *habitants* of Pointe Lévy to Ste Marie. One Sunday before Mass, they entered Claude Patry's house, next to the church, where a crowd had gathered. It was on this report that Monsr Jacqs Parant, who has always distinguished himself by his seditious remarks, judged it appropriate to go to the *Bostonnais* to tell them it was urgent to go warn common people.

On All Souls' Day [November 2], before and after Mass, the manifestoes, that the rebels had sent a few days prior to their arrival, were read to the people assembled by Capt. Parant and le sieur Dumergue in the houses surrounding the church.

This winter, Philipe Valière, first bailiff who behaved as a loyal subject for the public good and on the King's behalf, posted an order on the church door that the people were to mark their paths with some posts. Several *habitants* insulted him for issuing such orders, especially Jean Bilodau, the son, who rudely shouted at him "Where is he, your King? He is in town facing the mouth of a cannon."

The said Valière retorted that he did not acknowledge any authority but that of the King.

Jean Bilodau, the father, the beadle of the church, refused communion to the said bailiff, contrary to the priest's orders and the usual custom, because he had always conducted himself as a loyal subject of the King.[61]

Mr Taschereau's estate and mill have been ransacked this winter, sometime in February, by a certain Mach. On an alleged order from the said Arnold, [Mach] held a public auction of all the household goods, farm tools, and assets found on the property.

The named Robert served as interpreter, Claude Patry as bailiff, and Dumergue as recorder.

The majority of *habitants* of this parish and several from neighboring parishes went to this auction and purchased items.

The capt. of Ste Marie and the one from St François were also present at the auction and purchased items.

When Mr Taschereau gathered the *habitants* of this parish in the spring of 1775 to establish the militia and appoint a capt., a certain Louis Marcoux declared that they should wait and see how the other parishes conducted themselves.

Pierre Commiray also spoke very impertinently. No one in this parish took up arms for the rebels. Several have voluntarily made trips and [were?] paid [by?] the rebels when they passed through [the region].

Cited as disloyal subjects in this parish for having always spoken seditiously: Louis Gagné, the father, Jean Bilodau, the father, Antoine Marcoux, Jean Bte Grinier, Pierre Marcoux, Joseph Prou, Etienne Vachon, the father, Pierre Grinier, Pierre Poirier, Louis Marcoux, Jean Lefevre, Adrien Langevin, Vincent Commiray & c.

It seems that a number of *habitants* from this parish wanted to enter into some discussions with us before cheering, "Long live the King."

The named Jean Lefevre, Antoine Marcoux, Joseph Huard, and Julien Landry, the father, sent Pierre Poirier to speak on their behalf. As a result, we have condemned the said Pierre Poirier and the 4 others to ask forgiveness from the King on the following Sunday in front of the whole militia and also to apologize to a few loyal subjects for having scandalized them with their remarks. Bte Grinier suffered the same punishment for having maliciously said that an Indian had recently told him that if the *habitants* obeyed an order to take up arms, they would all be burned. The punishment was inflicted on June 29, following Mass in the presence of Monsr Taschereau and the whole militia; all cheered, "Long live the King" three times.

Left for St Joseph, Thursday, June 27 at 6:00 A.M.

Nouvelle Beauce—St Joseph Parish

Ministered by Mr Verreau.

Thursday, June 27.

The militia assembled at 10:00 A.M.

The reading of our charges.

Dismissal of:

Frans Lessard, capt., François Lessard, the son, lieut, and Louis Paré, ensign.

Discharge of the bailiffs.

Appointment of officers acknowledged by the reading of their commissions:

Pierre Poulin, Capt.

Alexdre Commiray, Lieut

Joseph Nadau

Joseph Poulin, the son

Pierre Poulin, the son } Sergeants

André Bisson

Reviewed 83 men.

Public address. [Cheered] "Long live the King" & c.

COMMENTS

When Mr Taschereau arrived in May 1775 to establish the militia as in Ste Marie, this parish unanimously revolted and refused to acknowledge the King's authority, despite the good counsel of their priest. He used all of his influence to have them comply and was insulted several times on this occasion. When Monsr Taschereau tried to approach the crowd, the people dispersed, refusing to hear him. This parish immediately sent Bazil Vachon *dit* Pomarlau and Giguère down to Ignace Ferland's house, Ste Marie's bailiff. They tried to convince him to go to every house in the parish to persuade the *habitants* to side with them, which the bailiff refused to do. The episode is recorded at Mr Dunn's house.[62]

Monsr Dunn sent the commissions with the names of the above-mentioned officers to the priest, who read them aloud in front of the parish. The aforesaid officers did not think it appropriate to accept [the commissions] and returned them to Mr Dun[n], who sent them right back with orders that they had to accept them. They have not only refused to serve as officers, but also have acted and spoken in favor of the rebels.

Spies have repeatedly passed through this parish last summer without meeting the slightest opposition.

Several times Ensign Louis Paré read the manifestoes that the rebels had sent shortly before their arrival.

When the rebels passed through this parish, the *habitants* helped them most willingly. The majority of them provided the rebels with canoes and received payment for taking them down the river.

Last February, the named Mach demanded from Frans Nadau, the parish miller who works for La Gorgendière's heirs and is a great friend of the rebels, the wheat and money that he held for Mr Taschereau.[63] Nadau complied without the least resistance. He also gave Mach the money that the said miller well knew that the said le sieur Taschereau had only received by proxy.

Capt. Frans Lessard behaved in the same manner towards the said Mach for money that belonged partly to Mr Taschereau and partly to La Gorgendière's heirs.

The said Mach was accompanied by Robert, Claude Patry and Dumergue.

Cited as the worst subjects, the Lessards, the Labés, the Pomarlaus, Louis Paré, Sans Soucy, the Cloutiers, especially Prisque Cloutier, Gervais Champagne, Prisque Doyon and Frans Nadau, the father.

In general, this parish's spirit has always leaned towards the rebels.

Joseph Champagne was cited in the journal for St Nicolas and Gervais Houle in that of Ste Marie.

The same for Jacques Ducharme, who all during the winter behaved as a [loyal] subject renouncing his errors.

St François Seigniory—Annex of St Joseph Parish

Reviewed 22 men.

The former officers and the bailiffs were not present, and, in their absence, it was impossible to make a report about the situation of this parish and of its officers. We told them that we were discharging the bailiffs and that orders would come, until further notice, from the officers who had been

View of Cape Diamond from the River S. Lawrence, by George Heriot. Courtesy of the National Archives of Canada (C-12774).

appointed last fall: Frans Quirion, capt., Joseph Lecadien, lieut, and Joseph Veilleu, ensign.

N.B. This parish needs to be kept under close watch.

Left for Ste Marie at 5:00 P.M.

Messieurs Baby and Williams left for Quebec, Friday, June 28.

Monsr Taschereau left for Quebec, Monday, July 1.

Left for Pointe Lévy on Friday, July 5, at 1:00 P.M.

Pointe Lévy

Parish priest, Mr [Jean-Jacques] Berthiaume.

Friday, July 5.

The militia assembled at 3:00 P.M.

The reading of our charges.

Called forth and discharged Joseph Lambert for reasons that we will give later.

Called and discharged:

Joseph Samson
Baptiste Bejin

Discharge of the bailiffs.

We have announced that this parish has, in general, behaved very treacherously and that we could not find, at present, worthy subjects to appoint as officers for the King. We have deemed it appropriate to leave in place the following, until it pleases His Excellency General Carleton to order otherwise:

François Bourassa, Capt.   for the company of the lower
Jacques Bejin, Lieut   section of the parish

Etienne Bejin, assistant <u>captain</u>, to serve as captain in the company of the upper section of the parish.

Public address as usual. [Cheered] "Long live the King" & c.

Reviewed   84 men upper company
              43 men lower company

COMMENTS

Le sieur <u>Joseph</u> Lambert had been appointed captain for the King last fall. He served the rebels in this rank until January, and then was continued in their service by an assembly of his company ordered by Congress.

He served the rebels in this rank with so much zeal and enthusiasm until their defeat, that his fellow parishioners blamed and denounced him openly, although almost all were disloyal subjects.

He was not present at the review being ashamed, we were told, of his past disloyal conduct.

We were told that he had turned in the commission that he had received from the rebels to General Carleton. Although absent, we have declared him guilty and unfit to ever hold any government position.

Joseph Samson was made capt. of the company of the lower section for the rebels by an election of this company.

Baptiste Bejin had been appointed Joseph Lambert's lieutenant in the same fashion.

Both proved their zeal for the rebels on repeated occasions.

We have declared them unworthy of holding any government position & c.

Joseph Samson told us that he had turned in to General Carleton the commission that he had received from the rebels.

Baptiste <u>Bejin</u> said that he never received one [commission].

Last fall, le sieur Frans Bourassa had been appointed capt. for the King, le sieur Jacques Bejin, his lieut, and Etienne Bejin, Joseph Lambert's lieutenant. They had the rebels' orders carried out, in their ranks as officers, until Congress ordered the parish to appoint others.

It does not seem that they have willingly served the usurpers of this parish. They even denounced rather openly a few of the most disloyal individuals in this parish.

Before the rebels arrived at Pointe Lévy, they always showed themselves as zealous servants of the King and opposed sedition and mutiny in this parish.

Those named below were the most mutinous and seditious at the tumultuous assembly that was held here last fall. When the government sent officers to invite this parish to side with the King, they sent envoys to invite people in neighboring parishes to join them in resisting the government's approach and stood guard until the rebels arrived.

Augustin Allé, the father
Fanchon Carier
Barras Lecour
Charles Guay
Charles Leguay *dit* Lenoir
Ambroise Lecour
Janot Guay's son
Ignace Couture

The named Ayot[te] from Kamouraska was captain here of a company formed from young men of different parishes. The rebels paid them 48 # per month. They stood guard and worked at the battery.

This company lasted about 6 weeks.

Here are the names of those who belonged to it from this parish:

Jean Carier's son
Bte Paradis's son
Etienne St Laurent
Michel Lecour
Charles Brulot *dit* Gezeron
Joseph Allé *dit* Racapé
Chs Bejin's son
Louis Lemieux's son
Augustin Morin
Michel Couture's son

There are some others whose names it will be easy to establish.

Those named below have marched with the *Bostonnais* against the King's detachment under the command of Mons Beaujeu and participated in the action at Rivière du Sud at Michel Blay's house. It should be noted that they made this march without being forced:

Joseph Lièvre
Joseph Carier
Augustin Protin *dit* Couture
A son of Jean Carier
A do of Louis Carier
A do of André Carier
Joseph Allé's grandson

Ignace Carier
Louis Carier, dead
Frans Guay, Louis's son
Joseph Allé *dit* Racapé
Augn Allé
Saint Hilaire
Bazil Nolin

We think that there were some others whose names we do not have.

When the rebels arrived, Ignace Couture ran through the countryside to get them provisions, and he went out to meet them in La Beauce to urge them to come to Pointe Lévy's aid.

Jean Amelin and Joseph Couture cut parts for the battery in front of the town.

Several *habitants* of this parish collectively made two thousand fascines for the rebels' battery at a price of 48 # each hundred, but only got receipts for payment.

The rebels had a magazine here with supplies that were brought from the different parishes, and the people from this seigniory transported them to their [the rebels'] headquarters.

Almost all the *habitants* stood guard here last fall before the arrival of the *Bostonnais* to resist all the maneuvers that the Quebec garrison could have undertaken.

This parish was generally seditious and opposed to the King's orders; in summary, zealous and very fond of the rebels.

Left for Beaumont at 7:00 A.M., Saturday, July 6.

Beaumont

Ministered by Mr [Antoine Huppé *dit*] Lagroix.[64]

Saturday, July 6.

The militia assembled at 10:00 A.M.
The reading of our charges.
Dismissal of:

Joseph Couture Belrive, Capt.
Jean Moleur *dit* Lallement ⎫
Alexandre Fournier ⎭ Sergeants

Discharge of the bailiffs.
Appointment of officers acknowledged by the reading of their commissions:

Josh Roy, Capt.
Jos. Alexis Mignot Girard, Lieut

Charles Girard
Etienne Turgeon }   Sergeants
Ignace Adam

Reviewed 71 men.

Public address. [Cheered] "Long live the King" & c.

Called forth and complimented Augustin Fraser for his zeal, affection and loyalty for the King's service, assuring him that if his trade of roadmender was not incompatible with the rank of officer, he would have been appointed.

COMMENTS

Joseph Couture Belrive had been appointed capt. last fall by order of General Carleton. We have cashiered him because, in truth, out of weakness he had his two sergeants carry out the rebels' orders to have the people perform corvées. Last fall, his son and almost the whole parish took up arms at the invitation of Pointe Lévy's *habitants* to join with them and several other parishes in resisting the King's orders.

Capt. Belrive's son, Gosselin from Ste Anne, and Lièvre from Pointe Lévy went on a reconnaissance tour up to Pointe à la Caille two days before the battle at Michel Blay's.[65] They returned immediately to warn the Pointe Lévy camp that there was a royalist force readying against them. Belrive's son stayed home. Gosselin and Lièvre went with the rebels to capture the men standing guard at Michel Blay's house.

In March, Louis Vien, the father, Louis Vien, the son, Jean Couture, Guillaume Couture, Jacques Turgeon, Baptiste Fournier, Chs Labrie from Ville Marie and eight others, all armed, went to St Michel's mill to capture a certain Chasson. He had made a trip in town and was ready to return there on Mr Bojeu's [Beaujeu] orders with Sebastien Ouelet from Ste Anne. The above-mentioned captured him and kept him until they could turn him over to the rebels.

The named Joseph Alexis Mignot Girard, whom we had appointed lieutenant, was also captured by the rebels as a suspect and informant who helped the said Chasson and all those loyal to the King.

Bazil Nolet bore arms at Pointe Lévy for several weeks.

It does not seem that any *habitants* of this parish participated in the incident at Michel Blay's house. The next day, 8 or 10 members of this parish were ordered to take their carts and lead a rebel detachment to Blay's house. This parish had already executed a few other corvées at various times.

Left for St Charles at 2:00 P.M.

N.B. With the exception of 5 or 6 loyal subjects this parish very much tasted the spirit of rebellion and always showed zeal for the rebels.

St Charles

Parish priest, Mr [Louis] Sarrault [Sarault].

Saturday, July 6.

The militia assembled at 3:00 P.M.

The reading of our charges.

We have called forth and dismissed Louis Bernard Gontier for reasons that we will explain later.

<u>Discharge of the bailiffs</u>.

Appointed and commissioned as officers:

Joseph Royer, Capt.
Jos. Izidore Doiron, Lieut
Jean Bilodeau ⎤
Ignace Ruel ⎥
Jean Bte Pasquet ⎥
Jean Lacasse ⎬ Sergeants
Louis Godebou ⎥
Louis Gosselin ⎦

Public address as usual.
Reviewed 160 men. [Cheered] "Long live the King" & c.

COMMENTS

Louis Bernard Gontier had received a captain's commission for the King last summer. He was very loyal for a time, trying to follow the government's orders to recruit ten men per one hundred. A number of *habitants* of this parish arrested him and held him captive from morning to night in Etienne Couture's house; but he quickly changed his conduct. He was at Pointe Lévy with the majority of this parish. It is true that he stayed at Jean Guay's house in the said parish and that he did not personally attend the tumultuous assembly that took place there. He issued orders to the *habitants* to go stand guard at Beaumont.

Upon a request from two rebel officers, he visited a few houses to say that these two men were searching for people of good will to go south to fight the King's militia.

Note. There have been no lower ranked officers appointed in this parish, and the rebels did not appoint any during the winter.

This winter, an Acadian and a Canadian from Ayot[te]'s company came to retrieve a few bottles of wine and a complete outfit of clothing from Mr Fraser's house.[66]

Frans Leclaire
Joseph Gosselin
Jos. Jean Gosselin
Ambroise Nadau
Joseph Mitron,

have been the most opposed to the government and have the greatest responsibility for stirring up the people last summer. They have almost always spoken in favor of the rebels. They kept saying that it was necessary to go help them [the rebels] take Quebec after the December 31 episode.

At the church door, François Leclaire read a letter from Congress to the Canadians urging them to continue their friendship.

British troops in Canadian winter dress. Uniforms of the American Revolution: 21st Regiment of Foot—Winter in Canada, 1776–1777. Watercolor by Charles MacKubin Lefferts, Accession number 1921.112, Negative number 16633. Courtesy of the Collection of the New-York Historical Society.

Poliquain's son
Jolin's son
One of Joseph Lepage's children
One of Chatilly's children

have been at the rebels service for some time at Pointe Lévy for 40 # per month.

Last fall, part of this parish went to Beaumont as corvée to stand guard for 8 or 10 days to resist the incursions that they suspected the King's troops would make.

They were armed with rifles.

Almost all of them had attended the seditious gathering at Pointe Lévy last fall but apparently without arms.

During the winter, they went to sell their food to the rebels at Pointe Lévy. Some of them have been as far as Ste Foye.

Left for St Michel at noon.

St Michel

Parish priest, Mr [Antoine Huppé *dit*] Lagroix.

Sunday, July 7.

The militia assembled at 2:00 P.M.

The reading of our charges.

Discharge of Baptiste Roy, first bailiff and commissioned capt. by Genl Carleton on June 9, 1775.

The same for:

Jean Pilot
Michel Montminy   Sergeants
Eloy Roy

We have been unable to get enough information to identify the good subjects from the bad. After having cashiered the above-mentioned, we have renewed the bailiffs in their rank until new orders are issued:

Claude Boulanger
Augustin Pilot
Eloy Roy

COMMENTS

We have cashiered Capt. Baptiste Roy and the above-mentioned sergeants. In their roles as officers, [they] had the rebels' orders carried out, particularly for having signal fires built, tended, and guarded in turn by armed *habitants* who followed his [Roy] orders. Last fall, he went with a large number of parishioners to join the *habitants* of Pointe Lévy in the tumultuous assembly that they held.

After this assembly, the *habitants* of this parish stood guard to resist the government's punishment that they feared they would receive. They occupied the presbytery and turned it into their guardhouse.

Noël Racine, the father, cited as one of the most infamous rebels from St Michel.

The same for Joseph Rouillard, Jean Racine, the son, Louis Racine, the son, Pierre Larochelle, Jean Pilote, Ignace Fortin, the son, who were all present at the March 25 episode at Michel Blay's house. Joseph Fortin, the son of the former Capt. Fortin, seems to have been there by chance after the incident.

This parish, in general, resisted the King's orders and showed support for the rebels.

N.B. They lit three fires in this parish to signal that ships were approaching.
Reviewed 118 men.

Public address. [Cheered] "Long live the King" & c.

St Valier [Vallier]

Paris priest, Monsr [Charles] Garrault [Gareault].

Monday, July 8.

The militia assembled at 9:00 A.M.
The reading of our charges.
We have called forth and cashiered the following:

Pierre Bouchard, Capt. for the King
Jean Valier Boutin, Lieut ditto
Jacques Coriveau
Baptiste Breton
René Laverdière
Etienne Remillard ⎬ ditto [Sergeants]

Nominated and commissioned as officers:

André Aubé, Capt.
Germain Blondau, Lieut
Pierre Aubé
Jean Blondin
Joseph Lacombe   }   Sergeants
Joseph Mari Roulau
Pierre Noël Laverière

Discharge of the bailiffs.
Public address as usual.
Reviewed 119 men. [Cheered] "Long live the King" & c.

COMMENTS

Pierre Bouchard allowed his house to serve as the guardhouse for the *habitants* for two or three days last fall. They intended, by this conduct, to protect themselves from the incursions that they supposed that the town's militia would make.

Around the end of last April, the said Pierre Bouchard, on the rebels' behalf, also was bold enough to order the *habitants* to bring wood to build three signal fires to warn them if ships approached. He also ordered three armed men to stand guard daily for four or five days. Only one of these fires was actually built.

Jean Valière [Valier] Boutin worked with Pierre Bouchard in overseeing these fires.

It is good to note that both of them had been singled out by His Excellency General Carleton because of their conduct, having received the commissions of capt. and lieut for this parish last May 15.

The sergeants acted with zeal for the rebels tending the fires, except for Etienne Remillard who seems to have been forced by Pierre Bouchard.

On Friday, May 3, the named Clément Gosselin, in the rebels' service, ordered a parish assembly during which Louis Beaugis was appointed capt., the named Langevin, lieut, and Julien Mercier, ensign.[67]

The widow Gabourie, nicknamed "the Queen of Hungary," caused more harm in this parish than anyone. She often held and presided over gatherings in her house, raised the people's spirit against the government, and urged them to side with the rebels. To ensure better success of her despicable plan, she served them strong drinks.

The named Louis Baugis [Beaugis], Pierre Lepage, Julien Mercier, Joseph Corivau, bonhomme François Richard and his son (these last 4 were jailed in Quebec in May and then freed by Genl Carleton) showed great stubbornness against the King's cause and much zeal for the rebels.

Jean Bazin and the named Taillon (the latter a *habitant* from Pointe Lévy) forced le sieur Germain Blondeau from his home, took him to Louis Beaugis's house, where he was held captive for three days and then transferred to the Pointe Lévy camp.

A certain Lapointe received the same treatment from Jean Bazin and Taillon.

Messrs Blondin and Chasson were captured by Julien Mercier.

Here are the names of those who were against the King's militia at Michel Blay's house:

François Leclaire
Two sons of a certain Silvin
François Boucher
Michel Richard
Joseph Corivau, son of bonhomme Corivau
Baptiste Laflame
Pierre Lepage
[no name] Baugis
Pierre Noël Laverrière
Bazil Fortier
the two sons of Jean Montigny

Joseph Marcoux, enlisted at Etienne Lapiere's
Nicolas Fradé
A certain Cretien enlisted at Michel Blay's house
Joseph Morin *dit* Miscou
Joseph Martin
François Thibault
Jean Bte Thibault
Jean Saintonge

Those listed below transported to Pointe Lévy 100 measures of wheat that they seized for the rebels from Mad. Lanaudière's mill.[68]

Jacques Belanger
Frans Acelin
Ustache Fortin
Michel Telier
Ustache Roy
Nicolas Fradé

They have received a certificate for payment.

The named Pierre Lepage and Beaugis left to join the rebels for the Blay incident, but they arrived too late. The action was over.

Last fall, the great majority of the parish went to the seditious assembly at Pointe Lévy and afterwards stood guard in this parish fearing the arrival of royal troops. Last spring, they built three signal fires upon the rebels' orders to warn them of the arrival of ships. They had armed *habitants* guard these fires.

During the winter, they brought their goods to Pointe Lévy and sold them to the rebels.

Left for Berthier at 1:00 P.M.

Berthier

Ministered by Mr [Pierre-Laurant] Bédard.

Monday, July 8.

The militia assembled at 3:00 P.M.
The reading of our charges.
Discharge of the bailiffs.
Appointment of officers:

Eloy Mercier, Capt.
Pascal Corivau, Lieut
François Mercier ⎫
Jean Mercier ⎬ Sergeants
Bte Blay, the son of Bte ⎭

Reviewed 64 men.
Public address. [Cheered] "Long live the King" & c.

COMMENTS

Last fall, this parish, particularly the upper section, opposed the nomination of officers for the King in their parish.[69]

Joseph Morancy, first bailiff, is cited as one of the most seditious subjects of this parish.

Last fall, he had most of the *habitants* of this parish accompany him to the seditious and riotous assembly at Pointe Lévy. He and a group of others went there. Another group, having met some people who were returning from the assembly, decided to turn back and return home themselves.

Following the assembly, this parish stood guard to resist the government, fearing new orders or reprisals. One group stayed at Germain Beaudoin's house, another at Jacques Lavoye's, and a third in the Cove of Bellechasse, where the bailiff himself stayed.[70] The said Morancy, the bailiff, either upon orders or because of his zeal, having learned that a group of royalists was forming below, established a guard of 15 or 20 men under his own command at Roderich McEndire's house. The names are:

Basil Dion
Louis Nadau
Jean Nadau
Louis Fortier, a boy
Jacques Boutin
Joseph Provençal & c.

Janot Nadau
Jacques Blanchet
Joseph Lessard
Jean Isabel
Joseph Lemieux, the son

Jean Nadau, having knowledge that Donald MacKinnon had gone to observe the scouts who had gone to Pointe à la Caille, whom we mentioned in the Beaumont journal, and suspecting that the said Donald McKinnon [MacKinnon] would go warn the royalists, made his report to Joseph Morancy.[71] He [Morancy] sent Jean Nadau, Joseph Lessard, Louis Nadau, Jacques Boutin, and Joseph Lemieux to his [MacKinnon] house and had him taken into custody.

Joseph Morancy, bailiff
Louis Nadau
Le Cadien (deserter)
Jacques Boutin, the son
André Lavoye
Michel Lacombe
Joseph Lemieux
Bazil Dion
Louis Dion
Jean Nadau
Chs Morancy Butau
Gabriel Bedouin

these people were found
at Blay's house during
and after the action.

The said Joseph Morancy, after taking part in the March 25 episode, went to Mr Cunot's house the next day and arrested le sieur [Jean-Bernard]

Duberger [Dubergès], the surgeon, who was tending Mr [Charles-François] Baillif's [Bailly's] wounds at the time.[72] He refused to give the said Duberger enough time to finish tending his patient's wound and treated him very harshly, as he did Mr Bailli [Bailly]. Overall, he was a very disloyal subject from beginning to end and gave repeated proofs of it. It was upon his orders that the signal fires were built. Almost all of the *habitants* of this parish tended and guarded the said fires.

In the beginning of May, upon Clément Gosselin's orders, the parish appointed François Chrétien as capt. and Joseph Morancy as lieutenant.

Noted as bad subjects: Bte Blay, Augustin's son, Augustin Blay, the son, Griffard, Dubord's farmer, Joseph Charité and his father, & c.

This parish always showed much affection for the rebels, especially the upper section.

Left for St François [du Sud] at 6:00 P.M.

St François du Sud

Parish priest, Mr [Pierre-Laurant] Bédard.

Tuesday, July 9.

The militia assembled at 9:00 A.M.

The reading of our charges.

Called forth and discharged:

Pierre Morin, Capt. for the King
Joseph Gervais, Lieut do
Louis Thibault ⎫
Jean Frans Picard ⎬ Sergeants do
Joseph Dumas ⎭

We called forth and publicly shamed the following officers appointed upon the rebels' orders:

Pierre Butau, Capt.

Joseph Dumas, Ensign

Bapte Forgeau ⎤

Louis Thibault ⎦   Sergeants

Discharge of the bailiffs.

We have appointed and commissioned as officers:

Louis Blay, Capt.

Pierre Boissonnau *dit* Saintonge, Lieut

Ignace St Pierre ⎤

Jacqs Gendron, the son of Jacques ⎬   Sergeants

Prisque Laprise ⎦

Reviewed 46 men.

Public address. [Cheered] "Long live the King" & c.

COMMENTS

Pierre Morin had an order from the rebels posted on the church doors.

At Berthier, he received from a certain Clément Gosselin an order from the rebels. They demanded that the *habitants* of this parish, on pain of being pillaged and burned, join them in marching against the King's detachment at St Pierre. Upon his arrival he [Morin] gave this order to his sergeant, Joseph Dumas, and he [Dumas] spread the news to only a few households. It is noted that he [Morin] returned here from Berthier with the above-mentioned Gosselin and the named Ayot[te]. These two men gathered a group of parishioners to stand guard for the night.

He followed the rebels to St Pierre but does not seem to have been involved in the battle.

Joseph Gervais kept refusing to accept an ensign's commission for the King, fearing the resentment of his countrymen.

The above-mentioned sergeants have served the rebels in their respective rank.

The said Noël Laplanche shouted at the door of the church that those who were in favor of Congress should gather at Moise Morin's house. Most of the people went and drafted a petition requesting permission to appoint officers. Moise Morin and Pierre Butau were entrusted to carry it to the rebels' camp. In response, they summoned another assembly of *habitants* at which Clément Gosselin presided. They nominated the officers whom we have already cited.

The ones we mention below were the most rebellious and the most supportive of the King's enemies; those who ordered a guard for Berthier in the fall; those who, fully armed, stopped the food supplies that le sieur Prou bought for Quebec in the fall and redirected it to the rebels' army:

Pierre Forgeau	Jacques Morin
Noël Laplanche	Pierre Butau
Joseph Dumas	

Here are the names of those who have marched against the King's detachment at St Pierre:

Pierre Forgeau
Noël Laplanche and his son
Jacques Gendron, the son of François
Joseph Boulet

Remainder of those who have been with the rebels against the King's detachment at St Pierre:

Joseph Blay
Jean Morin, the son of Moise
Jacques Robert
François Beaudoin
Isaac Gervais
Pierre Leclaire

Jean Boulet Rondau

François Boulet

Pierre Butau and his son Joseph

Jean Alaire

Julien Pigeon

Lamotte Garant

Joseph Dumas

Jacques Morin Ducharme

Jean Frans Picard

Antoine Morin, the son of Jean

Louis Morin

Louis Thibault

Michel Laflame

Joseph Gendron

Antoine Lachaîne

His son Antoine do

Joseph Laflame

Pierre Morin

Moise Morin, the father

Robert Boulet, the father

Louis Glasson and his son Jean Baptiste

Ustache Ch. Ouimare

Alexis Blanchet

Augustin Picard

Ignace Terrien

René Laprise

Michel Acelin

Jean Boulet *dit* Matelot

François Gendron, the son, is the only one from this parish who went to join Mr Beaujeu.

Almost half of this parish went to the seditious assembly at Pointe Lévy last fall and stood guard at Berthier. During the winter, they went to sell their goods at Pointe Lévy and Ste Foye.

Left for St Pierre [du Sud] at 3:00 P.M.

St Pierre du Sud

Parish priest, Mr [Jean-François] Curot.

Wednesday, July 10.

The militia assembled at 1:00 P.M.

The reading of our charges.

Called forth and cashiered the following officers appointed for the King last fall for reasons that we will give later. We declared them unworthy of ever holding any government position:

Louis Fontaine, Lieut
Joseph Morin, Ensign
Prisque Laprise
Augustin Blanchet   }   Sergeants
Joseph Valière

We publicly shamed and declared unfit to serve the government:

Jean Blanchet, Capt.	appointed by parish election during an
Augustin Morin, Lieut	assembly ordered by Clémt Gosselin,
Jean Dessince *dit*	who presided over the meeting held in
St Pierre, Ensign	April at Augustin Morin's house.

Discharge of the bailiffs.

We have reappointed and nominated as officers:

Michel Toussaint Blay, Capt.
Michel Blay, the son, Lieutenant

Antoine Talbote *dit* Gervais
Louis Pellerin
Pierre Blanchet, the son of Louis
Jean Blay, the son of Joseph

} Sergeants

Routine public address to the officers to recommend that they show equity, but above all, firmness; to arrest anybody who would make disparaging remarks towards the government; to maintain the roads in good repair & c.

Reviewed 91 men. [Cheered] "Long live the King" & c.

COMMENTS

Louis Fontaine was seen bearing arms on the evening of the action at Michel Blay's house. He was coming from St François to get powder and a keg of brandy upon orders from the named Ayot[te]. On Holy Saturday [April 6], he assembled the parish at his home upon the rebels' orders and asked if any parishioner wanted to enlist for 40 # per month. The seven individuals named below accepted this offer. They left for Pointe Lévy, where they have served until the moment that the rebels fled. They have returned here.

Joseph Ayot[te]
Jean Bte Monmeny
One of Jean Marot's children
Beaupré Cloutier
the named Gauvin
Augustin Picard
Noël Gagné

Joseph Morin told the sergeant who was ordering him to join the King's detachment that he would not march for or against the King; his sentiments were for the rebels in the action at Michel Blay's.

Augustin Blanchet, after having ordered that people join Mr Beaujeu's detachment, went with the said Jean Dessaince [Dessince] *dit* St Pierre to warn the rebels of this development and returned with their army. However, he was not seen at the battle.

Pierre Laprise	have acted in their rank as sergeants for the
Germain Morin	rebels and marched, as we will show, against
Joseph Valière	Michel Blay, except for Pierre Laprise.

Augustin Morin had 60 measures of wheat taken from Joseph Blay's house and 50 from Louis Fontaine's. It seems, however, that the owners did not object much. He [Morin] had the parishioners bring this wheat to the rebels at Pointe Lévy. All those involved got only a receipt as payment.

Below are the names of those who most opposed the government, took part in inciting the parish, and rendered the most assistance to the rebels.

Augustin Morin
Pierre Morin
Augustin Rousseau
Jean Dessaince [Dessince] *dit* St Pierre
Jacques Picard
Augustin Blanchet
Charles Cloutier

Names of those from this parish who joined the rebels against the King's militia in the action at Michel Blay's house on March 25.

Jacques Picard
Antoine Morin, his two sons and his nephew Louis Fontaine
Ignace Letournau
Alexandre Blanchet and his two sons
Marchetere, working at Augusn Bouchard's house
Jean Bte Chartier
Germain Morin
François Cloutier, the son of Gabriel

Augustin Roussau

Jean Roussau

Joseph Valière

Jean Izabel, the son

Augustin Mathieu

Louis Marie Picard

André Picard

Joseph and Jean Martin

René Mathieu

Charles Mathieu, the son and his father

Bazil Picard

Paul Marot

Augustin Picard

Augustin Morin

Jean Bte Arnois

Pierre Picard

Jean Dessaince [Dessince] *dit* St Pierre and his son

Augustin Valière

Augustin Gervais

Joseph Lavaigne

Joseph Ayotte

Joseph Gervais

Charles Cloutier

Jean Bte Montmeny working for Joseph Morin.

The following have received pay from the rebels for a certain time:

Louis Gagnon

Cormark Écossais

Charles Cloutier, the son of Joseph

François Blanchet, Alexandre's son

Antoine Izabel

American soldier from a regiment that served in Canada under Richard Montgomery. Uniforms of the American Revolution: 3rd N.Y. Regiment, 1775. Watercolor by Charles MacKubin Lefferts, Accession number 1920.147, Negative number 16647. Courtesy of the Collection of the New-York Historical Society.

Joseph Ayotte
Laurent Cloutier's eldest son

Michel Blay, the father, and Michel Blay, his son, are the only individuals from this parish who have been looted by the *Bostonnais*, as well as by the Canadian rebels. This was after the March 25 episode. We have a report to support these facts.

The genuine proof of Michel Blay's zeal and affection for his King led us to decide to retain him as capt. of this parish, although he had a brief lapse, which we must here explain.

The named Ayotte from the lower coastal region, capt. for the rebels, came here last January and asked Capt. Michel Blay to announce at the church doors that those who wished to enlist for the Congress should come forward. Blay carried out this request but only with the intention of preventing any trouble. In fact, he presented the situation with such irony that nobody came forward.

You will find below the names of those from this parish who joined with Blay for the King.

Mr Baillif [Bailly], parish priest
Michel Blay, the son
Berthelemy Gagné
Louis Malbeuf
Julien Fontaine
Jean Blay, the son of Joseph
Hyacinthe Peltier
Jean Izabel, still in prison
Louis Pelerin
Antoine Talbot *dit* Gervais

There are only about 9 families in this parish who remained truly loyal to the government.

Almost all these parishioners have been to Pointe Lévy and to Ste Foye to sell their goods during the winter.

Ten to twelve went to the seditious assembly at Pointe Lévy last fall.

About 20 stood guard at Berthier, last fall, for almost a month.

Left for St Thomas at 3:00 P.M.

St Thomas

Parish priest, Mr [Jean-Baptiste] Maisonbasse.

Thursday, July 11.

The militia assembled at 9:00 A.M.

The reading of our charges.

We have called forth and cashiered, although absent, for reasons that we will give below:

Joseph Côté, Capt. for the King

We have publicly shamed and declared unworthy of ever holding any government position the following officers appointed by the rebels:

Joseph Lamonde, so-called Colonel

Jean Baptiste Picard ⎫
Joseph Boulanger ⎬ Officers
Victor Olivier ⎭

Several were absent

Thomas Fournier ⎫
Antoine Lamare ⎬ Sergeants

Called forth and cashiered Louis Thibault, appointed capt. by parish elections at the end of April.

Discharge of the bailiffs.

Nominated as officers and commissioned:

Jacques Thibault, Capt.
Jacques Nicol, Lieutenant
René Gagné, Ensign
François Mignau ⎫
Pierre Caron ⎪
Jacques Thibault, the son ⎬ Sergeants
Zachary Bonau *dit* Labécasse ⎪
Jean Baptiste Bernèche ⎭

Public address as usual.

Reviewed 121 men.

[Cheered] "Long live the King" & c.

COMMENTS

Joseph Côté, in his rank as captain, had the rebels' orders carried out and on different occasions gave proof of his zeal in serving them.

Those named below have been the most seditious in this parish. From the beginning, they incited the *habitants* to disobey the government's orders, ordered them to stand guard at Berthier in the fall and have done all they could to harass the militia commanded by Mr Beaujeu. In short, they have aided and assisted the rebels as much as they could.

Joseph Lamonde

Jean Bte Picard

Joseph Boulanger

Victor Olivier

Thomas Fournier

The named Levesque, notary in this parish, wrote petitions, which he had several *habitants* sign, inviting the rebels to come to this parish. He told the rebels that some royal supplies were stored in a few houses, one being the parish priest's, Mr Maisonbasse. It seems that upon his invitation, the rebels seized 3 barrels of Bordeaux wine in the said priest's house. In short, he [Levesque] has been very opposed to the government and to the small number of faithful subjects who live in this parish.

The following have been paid 40 # per month by the rebels:

Thomas Fournier's son

The son of the widow Prou from Rivière à la Caille

Dion from Rivière du Sud

Bazil Fournier

Clément Dépré, the son
One of Charles Lacombe's children.

You will find below the names of those from this parish who were for the King at the action at Michel Blay's house.

Desilets Couillard
Jacques Nicol
Joseph Thibault, the son
René Gagné
Basil Prou
Gaudrau du Bras
Augustin Dominique
[no name] Janot
Janot's wife's little boy, killed
Stellson, English, died from smallpox
Roger Thibault, the son

Louis Thibault, elected capt. by parish elections, had the baseness of accepting the commission. However, he does not seem to have had many opportunities to serve the rebels.

The following are those from this parish who were ready to march against the rebels upon Mr Beaujeu's orders.

Ebert Couillard
Bernard Duberger
François Mignau
François Gagné, the son of Joseph
Lesperance, the son
Belanger, the son of Felix's wife
Cardon Dambourgès
Jacques Thibault's boy

Joseph Couture
Baptiste Dupuis
Jean Desprès du Bras
Louis Gagné, the son of the widow Gagné du Bras
Cymare
Labécasse
Roger Gagner
François Boulet
Nicolas Metivier
Louis Dupuis
Louis Marie Thibault
Alexis Gosselin
Abel Michon

Last fall, the majority of the *habitants* of this parish stood guard here to prevent supplies from being transported to the town and to oppose the King's forces in case of a landing in this parish. Last fall, a few started to go to the seditious assembly at Pointe Lévy, but they returned to their homes having learned on their way that everyone was returning.

Most of them were opposed to the government and sympathized with the rebels.

Left for Cape St Ignace at 2:00 P.M.

Cape St Ignace

Ministered by Mr [Jacques] Hingan.

Thursday, July 11.

The militia assembled at 3:00 P.M.

The reading of our charges.

Dismissal of Augustin Bernier, capt., for reasons we shall give below.

Discharge of the bailiffs.

Appointment of officers:

Joseph Fournier, Capt.
Jean Bte Bernier, Lieut
François Guimont
Frans Dion, son of Joseph } Sergeants
François Lebreux
Joseph Lagacé

Reviewed 84 men.
Public address & c.

COMMENTS

Capt. Augustin Bernier was cashiered for having helped the rebels as much as he could with his seditious advice, his sympathy, and his vigilance in carrying out their orders with dispatch. He oversaw corvées, disseminated various publications, held parish assemblies in his own home to enlist them in the rebels' service, and tended and guarded the [signal] fires.

He swore an oath of allegiance to the rebels' service at the request of Clément Gosselin, who again had him acknowledged as capt. and withdrew the commission that he had received from General Carleton.

Louis Rigaut *dit* Bernier was appointed lieutenant at that same moment. Although he refused to take an oath, out of weakness he had some orders carried out in this role. Fear alone caused him to do so because previously he had shown affection and obedience for the government. He sent one of his children [to serve] under Mr Beaujeu's command.

Baptiste Dion was also appointed ensign by the said Clément Gosselin. Although he was absent at the time of the parish assembly, his zeal and affection for the rebels left no doubt about his acceptance [of the commission].

He enlisted with the rebels for 48 # per month, as did the named Joseph Gravel, Pierre Balar, one of the late Joseph Boulanger's children, Bte Boulé, Maurice Rodrigue, and a Gagné. François Fortin, the son of Louis, and a Forgeau went to St François du Sud to warn Forgeau Laplanche, the father of the said Forgeau, that a group of royalists was forming under Mr Beaujeu's command.

Cited as disloyal subjects:

Augustin Bernier, Capt.
Frans. René Fortin
[no name] Forgeau & c.
Baptiste Dion
Philipe Fortin
Denis Fortin

This parish showed strong sympathy for the rebels' cause and had refused to obey the King's orders last fall.

Le sieur Lebrun, the lawyer, displayed at times the conduct of a zealous subject and, at others, that of an extreme rebel.[73] This winter with Ferré, he ordered the confiscation of the wheat that Mr Duchesnay had in his St Roch seigniory, the product of his mill.[74] He [Lebrun] is strongly suspected of having given information to the rebels about Mons. Beaujeu's party while he was part of that group.

A small number of parishioners stood guard for the same reasons that we have explained in the journal previously.[75]

Names of those who marched against the rebels under Mr Beaujeu's orders:

Joseph Fournier
Jean Bte Bernier
Louis Fournier
Magloire Fournier
Ignace Lemieux, the son of Louis
Lazard Richard
François Rocher
Nicolas Silveste
One of Rigau Bernier's children
One of Jean Bte Bernier's do
Le sieur Lebrun

Benony Bernier, the son of the capt., since led the rebels upon his father's orders.

Left at 8:00 A.M. July 12 for Illette [L'Islet].

Illette [L'Islet]

Parish priest, Mr [Jacques] Hingan.

Friday, July 12.

The militia assembled at 9:00 A.M.

The reading of our charges.

Dismissal of Frans Xavier Caron for reasons that we shall give later.

Discharge of the bailiffs.

Appointment of officers:

Jean Bte Couillard Després, Capt.

Manuel Couillard Després, Lieut

Charles Fortin, Ensign

François Bernard ⎤

Paschall Mercier ⎟

Pierre Bouché   ⎬   Sergeants

Pierre Robichaud ⎦

Reviewed 130 men. Public address & c.

COMMENTS

We have discharged Capt. Frans Xavier Caron for having had the weakness of executing the rebels' orders and for having turned in his commission to Clément Gosselin, who had him acknowledged publicly as a capt. during a parish assembly this spring. During this assembly, he was made to swear a sort of loyalty oath to the rebels. However, he carried out Mr Beaujeu's orders to march against the rebels with zeal. We are convinced from the information that we have gathered that he only obeyed the rebels because of his old age and fear of threats made against him.

Last fall, this parish stood guard for the same reasons that the parish of Cape St Ignace did. They built fires and guarded them on Capt. Caron's orders.

Last fall, very few parishioners came forward [to volunteer] when required to establish the militia.

It seems that the spirit of neutrality reigns [in this parish].

The names of those who marched against the rebels upon Mr Beaujeu's orders:

Lebland, during the Blay episode
Germain Beaulieu
Frans Bernard
Marichon Caron
Nicolas Sanfaçon
Jean Desprès
[no name] Gaudrau
Joseph Lemieux
Frans Gagnon
and Pierre Picard, the son,

who afterwards enlisted with the rebels for 40 # per month. He received an advance of 4 piastres, but tricked them by never having left his house.

The names of those who enlisted with the rebels for 40 # per month:

Jacques Normand ⎫
Bone Normand   ⎬   for navigation
François Gaudrau ⎭

A Caron
Two sons of the late Frans Belanger
and Pierre Picard, the son, mentioned above.
Several individuals from this parish have brought food to sell to the rebels.
Left for St Jean [Port Joli] at 1:00 P.M.

St Jean Port Joli

Ministered by Mr [Jacques] Hingan.

Friday, July 12.

The militia assembled at 3:00 P.M.
The reading of our charges.
Dismissal of:

Guillaume Fournier, Capt.
Louis Fournier, Lieut
François Leclaire, Ensign,

for the reasons that we are giving below.
Discharge of the bailiffs.
Appointment of officers:

François Duval, Capt.
Charles Fortin, Lieut
Joseph Gagnon ⎤
Augustin Fournier ⎬ Sergeants
Louis Doustou ⎦

Reviewed [blank] men.
Public address & c.

COMMENTS

We cashiered Capt. Guillaume Fournier for, in his said rank, having the rebels' orders executed and, in truth, not through affection but fear. He carried out all of Mr Beaujeu's orders to serve the King with zeal and diligence and led his men to him at Pointe à la Caille. But since then, he has again carried out the rebels' orders to call assemblies to enlist men for their service. In truth, he refused to carry out his last orders, realizing his mistake. At this time, the parish, upon order of Clément Gosselin, called an assembly and nominated Julien Chouinard, a renowned and zealous rebel, as capt., Joseph Desrosiers, do, Jean Legüi and Laurent Caron as sergeants. We publicly shamed them all.

We cashiered Louis Fournier, the lieutenant, not only for having carried out the rebels' orders but also for having enlisted to serve with them for 40 # per month.

We have discharged François Leclaire, the ensign, for having, by order of Capt. Fournier, commanded for the rebels. Although, we learned from our source that he always showed great affection and obedience for the King's service.

Cited as disloyal subjects:

Julien Chouinard, Joseph Desrosiers, Dupuis, Forgeront, Jerome Dupuis, Janet Dechaine.

The fires were built and tended by order of Captain Chouinard.

The names of those who enlisted to bear arms in the rebels' service for 40 # per month:

Louis Fournier, Lieut
Antoine Laterreur, the son

The names of those who have joined Mr Beaujeu's corps:

Guillaume Fournier
Augustin Peltier
François Caron
Germain Beaulieu
Jean Marie Fortin
Jean Marie Chouinard
Frans Xavier Gagnon
McLoad
Lemieux
Jean Marie Duval
Joseph Labbé

Alexis Bellanger
Alexandre Fournier
Pierre Bellanger

This parish did not behave any better than the neighboring ones.
Left for St Roch at 6:00 P.M.

St Roch

Ministered by Mr [Pierre-Antoine] Porlier.[76]

Saturday, July 13.

The militia assembled at 9:00 A.M.
The reading of our charges.

François Peltier, Capt. Joseph Ouelet, Lieut Jacques Peltier, Ensign	They had been commissioned as sergeants for the King's service last summer. We have called them forth and discharged them for reasons that we will give below.

Basil St Pierre ⎫
Pierre Dubé ⎭ Sergeants

Discharge of the bailiffs.
Nominated and commissioned as officers:

Jean Morin, Capt.
Jean Marie Castonguay, Lieut
Chs Peltier ⎫
Pierre Bouchard ⎪
Ste Marie St Pierre ⎬ Sergeants
François Lizot ⎭

Public address as usual.
Reviewed 137 men. [Cheered] "Long live the King" & c.

French Canadian habitant *in winter dress, 1778, by Friedrich Von Germann. Courtesy of the Print Collection, Miriam and Ira D. Wallach Division of Art, Prints and Photographs, New York Public Library, Astor, Lenox and Tilden Foundations.*

COMMENTS

Last January, François Peltier received from Clément Gosselin and Ayot[te] an announcement whereby the rebels invited the *habitants* to take up arms and bring them supplies. He [Peltier] had the named Michau Morin read and then post [the announcement] at the church door.

He repeated this same operation several times later.

Upon le sieur Lebrun's demand, he [Peltier] had five carts transport part of the wheat that the rebels ordered stolen from Mr Duchesnay's mill. It was delivered to the said le sieur Lebrun's house at Cape St Ignace.

After the return of Mr Beaujeu's detachment, the rebels had him turn in his capt.'s commission to them and gave him one in Congress's name, which he accepted.

About a month later he turned it [the commission] over to a *Bostonnais* officer.

Last spring, he [Peltier] requisitioned carts for the rebels' service and had fires built to signal them when ships would arrive.

He disarmed Antoine Gerbère upon the rebels' orders.

It needs to be observed, however, that last fall the said François Peltier went with 6 other parishioners to offer their services to Mr Cramahé, who was good enough to give them certificates. He seems to have led Mr Beaujeu's detachment with much zeal. In short, it seems that he acted more out of weakness and timidity than from bad intent.

The officers and sergeants cited in the other part have been discharged for having aided and assisted François Peltier in carrying out rebel orders, in their respective ranks.

The named Ferré (with the help of Monsr Jean Bte Lebrun) went to seize about 110 measures of flour from Mr Duchesnay's mill and house.

Le sieur Metote, the brother-in-law of le sieur Lebrun, oversaw the measuring of this wheat. This was then transported to the said le sieur Lebrun's house in Cape St Ignace with carts taken from here, which they led with authority. Mr Duchesnay's miller, Joseph Queré, states that le sieur Lebrun threatened him saying that all the wheat that he had was needed. Le sieur Lebrun later sent him a receipt from the rebels for the 90 measures of flour that he [Queré] had delivered all at the same time.

Noël Peltier, the son	enlisted and served
Joseph Peltier, the son	at the rebels' camp
François Richard's son	for 40 # per month.

Below you will find the names of those from this parish who were for the King at the episode at St Pierre:

Joseph Morin, the boy, killed

Frans Morin, do

Jean Bte Duperé, the son

Joseph Duchaine's son
Joseph Marie Saussier
Pierre Blaise
Frans Peltier, the son of Jacques
Louis Peltier, the son of François
} They are still prisoners

Here are the names of those who have been with Mr Beaujeu to Pointe à la Caille:

Baptiste Dubé, the son of Pierre
Charles Blanchet
Louis Dupon, the son of Jacques
Joseph Ouelet
Michel Ouelet, the son of Frans
Benoist Lebel, the son of Roch
Jean Gagnon, the son of Jean
Michel Caron, the son of Joseph
Michel Gagon, the son of Michel Caron's wife
Joseph Larue
Jean Gerbère, the son of Jean
Caron, the son of Jean Marie Castonguay's wife
The son of the Big Joseph Ouelet
Chrisostome Ouelet
François Lassablonière
Joseph St Pierre
François St Pierre
Antoine Gerbère
Guillaume Lebel
Charles Peltier's son
Jean Morin

Upon the orders of le sieur Clément Gosselin, the parish made three fires to serve as a signal to the rebels upon the arrival of the ships.

Last fall, some stood guard here in an attempt to oppose the royalists if they would appear.

Louis Govin
The Big Joseph Ouelet

have been the most seditious, the most opposed to the government and the most devoted to the rebels' cause.

This parish, as a whole, seems to have been less rebellious than the others. Left for Ste Anne at 1:00 P.M.

Ste Anne

Parish priest, Mr [Pierre-Antoine] Porlier.

Saturday, July 13.

The militia assembled at 3:00 P.M.

The reading of our charges.

We have cashiered le sieur Augustin Roy *dit* Lauzier, captain for the King, due to his weakness for the rebels and his old age.

We also discharged Bte Peltier, ensign for the King, also on account on his weakness for the rebels; more specifically, for having commanded the named Chs Lagace, upon orders from Capt. Roy, to go with his cart to help transport wheat from Mr Duchesnay's house to le sieur Lebrun's at Cape [St Ignace] for the rebels.

Called forward and publicly shamed:

Germain Dionne, Capt. for the rebels
Joseph Soucy, Lieut do
Jean Aintel *dit* St Jean, Ensign do
Charles Lagacé ⎫
François Chrétien ⎪ Sergeants
Etienne Bohay ⎪
Pierre Quimpère ⎭

[Although some were absent, we have declared them all unworthy and unable of ever holding any government office]

Discharge of the bailiffs.
Nominated and commissioned as officers:

Augustin Roy, the son of *dit* Lauzier, capt., presently a prisoner
Bernard Lizot, Lieut
Jean Ouelet, Ensign
Louis Lauzier
Sebastien Ouelet
Gabriel St Pierre   } Sergeants
Moise Beaulieu

Public address as usual to recommend to the officers justice, but above all, firmness when executing the King's orders; to arrest any suspicious strangers, including women, should they speak against the government and in favor of the rebels; to keep roads in good repair; to invite the people to go to town as previously, & c.

Reviewed 94 men. [Cheered] "Long live the King" & c.

COMMENTS

We noted that les sieurs Augustin Roy and Bte Peltier have always shown much enthusiasm for the King's service and that it was only because of fear and ignorance that they strayed from their duty.

Germain Dionne and Clément Gosselin are two famous rebels who have aided and assisted the government's enemies in every way they could. They have stirred the people, enlisted them for the service of Congress, and ridiculed and threatened royalists.

The said le sieur Clément Gosselin was not content with carrying out this conduct only in this parish. He traveled to all of the others going as far as Pointe Lévy, preaching rebellion everywhere, inciting people to loot the small number of loyalists, and having them arrested. He read the rebels' orders and proclamations at the church door and forced some of the King's officers to do the same.

He posed as a traveling officer for Congress and, in this role, recruited and appointed some officers.

This well-known scoundrel, as well as Germain Dionne, has not been seen since the rebels' retreat.

The named Joseph Dionne, a notary, ordered an assembly to invite the people of this parish to enlist for the Congress.

He served as court clerk during the interrogation that Germain Dionne, his nephew, and Clément Gosselin, Germain Dionne's son-in-law, conducted after the escape of Mrs Riverin, Blondin, and Ferré.

Louis Gosselin	
Langlois Munier	
bonhomme Pasquet	are among the most seditious
Chs Lagacé	and most devoted to the rebels

Here are the names of those who enlisted in the rebels' service. Some were present at the action at St Pierre:

The two sons of bonhomme Pasquet
The 3 sons of the widow Pierre Deschaine
Germain Dionne's son
Bazil Lagacé
Antoine Chrétien
Germain Deplessi, the son
Augustin Dionne's son
Augustin Fournier
Frans Ayot
Louis Langlois
Louis Gosselin
Louis Morau
Gervais
Joseph Dionne's son

The small Jean Bohay

Gagné

The named [William] Ross, a Scot, has been assaulted repeatedly by the rebels.[77] They seized six cartloads of food from him. However, some claim that he had sold them the said food out of fear or to make a profit.

The said le sieur Ross, after the St Pierre action, left his house to avoid the rebels' pursuit. They had loaded the said le sieur Ross's schooner with a large amount of provisions that they found in his house. They took it to St Roch, where they hurriedly left it upon [hearing] the news that the King's vessels were approaching.

This schooner, with the provisions, was taken back to le sieur Ross's house a little later.

Below are the names of those from the parish who were for the King during the St Pierre episode:

Augustin Lauzier, the father
Augustin Lauzier, the son still prisoners
[no name] Duchouquet
Bernard Saussier
Pierre Chouinard
Jean Ouelet
[no name] Williams, English, prisoner
Joseph Francoeur
The two named Clermonts, woodworkers
A naval captain, wrecked at Mille Vaches, died from his wounds.[78]

Here are the names of those in this parish who remained with Mr Beaujeu at Pointe à la Caille:

The named Ross
Sébastien Ouelet
The named Degravier

The named Marot
Ross's servant
Bernard Lizot, the father
Bernard Saussier, the father
Antoine St Pierre
Thomas Lamy
Antoine Guy
Belonie Boutote
Jean Bte Lebrun
Jean Lafrance, the father
Gabriel St Pierre, the father

The *habitants* of this parish have helped transport supplies for the rebels, the majority of them, most willingly. Last fall, a few of them went to stand guard in the bay for one night only.

Left for Rivière Ouelle at 11:00 A.M.

Rivière Ouelle

Parish priest, Mr [Jean-Louis-Laurent] Parent.[79]

Sunday, July 14.

The militia assembled at noon.
The reading of our charges.
Discharge of:

Frans Gagnon, Capt.
Joseph Beaulieu, Lieut
Nicolas Beaulieu, Ensign
Pierre Boucher,
Assistant-major

All officers commissioned by Genl Carleton last summer, whom we discharged for the reasons that we will give below.

Discharge of the bailiffs.
Appointment of officers:

Joseph Boucher, Capt.

Ignace Boucher, Lieut

Jean Morais	
Antoine Beaulieu	
Joseph Martin	Sergeants
Jean Bte Bérubé	
Paul St Laurant	

Reviewed [blank] men.

Public address. [Cheered] "Long live the King" & c.

COMMENTS

We have indicated that, although absent, the named Bazil Dubé, commissioned by the rebels, aided and assisted them as much as he could, stirred the people, enlisted them for the Congress's service, ridiculed and threatened royalists & c. He also inspected the signal fires in all the parishes up to Rimousky.

We have indicated that Bonenfant, the son, (very impertinent and insolent) served the rebels most willingly as an assistant-major, appointed by the said Bazil Dubé. However, a short time later, he returned his commission at the solicitation of his wife and father.

We cashiered the above-mentioned Capt. François Gagnon who, in his said rank, willingly had all the rebels' orders carried out. Last winter, he wrote the rebels that he and his officers were able to serve and that there was no need to appoint new ones. He called assemblies to recruit people for the rebels' service. He also personally disarmed Jean Boucher after the March 25 episode.[80]

We have discharged his subordinate officers for having executed his orders in their respective rank. Nevertheless, from our information we recognize the assistant-major, Pierre Boucher, as a good and faithful subject of the government who gave proof of this on all occasions. He was one of the first men to march to Mr Beaujeu's party and, by his example and <u>advice</u>, enjoined his brothers and a few others to join him. But after this <u>good</u>

conduct, he had the weakness of commanding the execution of corvées and the maintenance of [signal] fires, by the orders of a rebel <u>captain</u>.

Names of those who enlisted with the rebels for pay this winter:

Augustin Lavoy, the son and his brother
Jean Bérubé, the son
Pierre Martin
Maurice Levesque
A certain Martin, the cousin of the first
Joseph Soucy and his brother
Louis Martin
Jean Martin
Etienne Perault
Augustin Peltier
Benjamin Deschaine
Frans Pinet

Furthermore, this spring Bazil Dubé enlisted 15 or 20 young men to help with navigation.

Last fall, Pierre Bérubé, Jean Levesque's two children (the said Jean Levesque being present), and Pierre Plourdre struck the assistant-major, Pierre Boucher, as he left Mass. Boucher served in the role of bodyguard for le sieur St Aubin, the notary. [Boucher was assaulted] for publicly reading an order from General Carleton.

Last fall, some *habitants* of this parish stood guard on the Pointe for the same reasons that the neighboring parishes did.[81]

As in the other parishes, the signal fires were built and tended on Bazil Dubé's orders.

Names of those who have marched under Mr Beaujeu's command this winter:

Pierre Boucher
Ignace Boucher

Joseph Boucher, wounded at the Blay episode
Jean Bte Boucher
Bazil Gagnon
Dominique Levesque's son
A Bérubé, the son of Michel Aumont's wife

Left for Kamouraska at 5:00 P.M.

We have left a blank page and resumed our journal in a small notebook.

Kamouraska

Parish priest, Mr [Joseph-Amable] Trutau [Trutaut].

The militia assembled at 9:00 A.M.

The reading of our charges.

We dismissed the militia and postponed the review until tomorrow at 8:00 A.M. for sound reasons.

Monday, July 15.

N.B. Since we had so much trouble establishing the truth after having held a session from 9:00 A.M. to noon, we have deemed it necessary to postpone the review until tomorrow in order to gather more information.

Left at 1:00 P.M. for Rivière des Caps.[82]

Rivière des Caps to Rimousky

Ministered by itinerant missionaries and sometimes by Kamouraska's parish priest, although he does not consider them his parishioners.

The militia assembled at 3:00 P.M. at Rivière des Caps.

The reading of our charges.

Monday, July 15.

Kamouraska

Parish priest Mr [Joseph-Amable] Trutau [Trutaut].

Tuesday, July 16.

The militia assembled at 8:00 A.M.

Dismissal of Alexandre Dionne, capt., Joseph Boucher, lieut, Alexis Nadeau, ensign, all officers from the First Company commissioned by General Carleton. We have discharged them for reasons that we shall give later.

The same for Benjamin Michaud, capt., Michel L'aîné, lieut, officers of the Second Company.

Discharge of the bailiffs.

New officers acknowledged by the reading of their commissions:

Alexandre Roy *dit* Dejardin, Capt.
Jean Bte Cureux St Germain, Lieut
Jean Lebel, Ensign

Ignace Roy Dejardin
Ignace Vaillancour
Etienne Tradiff
Augustin Lebel
Augustin Dionne   } Sergeants
Louis Vaillancour
Bastien Chassé
Joseph Levasseur, the son of Joseph

COMMENTS

The named Ayot[te] was appointed capt. for the service of Congress. He was one of the most infamous rebels in this province. He aided and assisted the enemies of the government in any way he could, stirred the people, recruited for the Congress, & c.

Last fall, Capt. Alexandre Dionne behaved as a zealous subject of the government. He marched to Pointe Lévy with several young men according to the orders that he had received to help the town [Quebec], but was unable to cross [the St Lawrence River] because all the canoes had already been removed by the town's people. This winter, he marched under the orders of Mr Beaujeu at the head of more than 30 men from his parish. Since that time, he has had the weakness to carry out the rebels' orders and had his subordinate officers and sergeants do the same in obedience to Bazil Dubé. In their service, he had signal fires tended and guarded, sent the search party for Mr Riverin's mare on the orders of Bazil Dubé, and had two letters delivered to pilots on the lower coast. In short, he has done all that he was asked. He is even accused of having pledged a loyalty oath to the said Bazil Dubé. All these reasons considered, we have dismissed him, as well as his subordinates.

We cashiered Benjamin Michaud, capt. of the Second Company, for having fires built and guarded in his district, for having made several orders for corvées for the rebels, and for allowing the letters to pass [through his district].

We cashiered Michel L'aîné, lieut, only for having delivered two letters to les sieurs Riou and Beaulieu, pilots. Capt. Alexandre Dionne had his sergeant, Joseph Morau, hand-deliver them with a recommendation to have the letters forwarded to the next captain. The said Michel L'aîné immediately asked one of his men to carry out the order. This sole weakness excepted, he always behaved as a loyal subject of the government and had previously served under Mr Beaujeu's command.

On orders of Ferré, the above-mentioned Capt. Alexandre Dionne once ordered a cart through his son and, on another occasion, drove one himself.

Names of those who enlisted with the rebels for 40 # per month.

Pierre Peltier
Amable Laplante
Jean Peltier
Augustin Lamare
[no name] Gilbert
Pierre Rivard
Jacqs Tardif
Jean Dubé

Pierre Chamare

Amant Landry

Alexandre Mignau

Joseph Morin

François Michaud and Louis Michaud, the sons of Joseph

Names of those who marched against the rebels under Mr Beaujeu's command:

Alexandre Dionne, Capt.

Michel L'aîné, Lieut

Alexandre Roy *dit* Dejardin

Jean Bte Cureux St Germain

Jean Lebel

Louis Michaud

Ignace Roy *dit* Dejardin

Pierre Duplessy, the son

Antoine Michaud, the son of Antoine

Jean Bte Roy *dit* Dejardin

Jean Nicolas *dit* Lebel

Joseph Choret

Bte Morau

Alexandre Levasseur

Michel Boucher

Jullien Ouelet

Frans Santier

François Cahouet

Antoine Michaud, son of Joseph

Jean Mador

Joseph Voizine

Pierre Rivard
Amable Laplante } have since enlisted in the rebels' service
Jaqs Tardif

Louis Corbin
Joseph Peltier
Joseph Ouelet
Pierre Lafériere
Pierre Landry
Bazil Lavoye
Jean Tardif
Benjamin Mador
Jean Peltier
Jean Perault
Jean Bois
Ignace Vaillancour

Left for Rivière Ouelle at 3:00 P.M.

Left Rivière Ouelle to spend the night in Pte à la Caille, Wednesday, July 17.

Left Pointe à la Caille for the review at St Michel at noon, July 18.

St Michel

The militia assembled at 2:00 P.M.

The reading of our charges.

Appendix

Itinerary of the Baby Journal

For those readers who are interested in doing further research on the Baby journal, this list shows the page numbers of the parish reports in both the original 1776 manuscript and the 1927 Fauteux edition.

PARISH	DATE INSPECTED	PAGE IN FAUTEUX	PAGE IN ORIGINAL
Vieille Lorette	May 22	435	3
Jeune Lorette	May 23	436	5
Charlesbourg	May 24	436	6
Beauport	May 25	437	9
L'Ange Gardien	May 25	438	11
Château Richer	May 26	439	13
Ste Anne	May 26	439	14
For St Féréol	May 26	440	15
St Joachim	May 27	440	17
Return to Château Richer	May 28	441	21
Ile D'Orléans—Ste Famille	May 28	442	23
Ile D'Orléans—St François	May 29	443	26
Ile D'Orléans—St Jean	May 29	444	28
Ile D'Orléans—St Laurent	May 30	445	32
Ile D'Orléans—St Pierre	May 30	446	35

PARISH	DATE INSPECTED	PAGE IN FAUTEUX	PAGE IN ORIGINAL
Returned to Quebec for the night			
Ste Foye	June 2	448	40
St Augustin	June 3	448	42
Pointe Aux Trembles	June 4	449	44
Ecureuils	June 4	450	47
Cap Santé	June 5	451	48
Deschambault	June 6	452	51
Les Grondines	June 6	453	54
Ste Anne	June 7	454	56
Batiscan	June 7	456	60
Rivière Batiscan, Ste Geneviève	June 8	457	64
Champlain	June 9	458	66
Cap La Madelaine	June 9	458	68
To Trois Rivières	June 9–14	459	70
Bécancour	June 15	459	71
Gentilly	June 15	461	76
St Pierre des Becquets	June 16	462	78
St Jean de L'Echaillon	June 16	464	83
Lotbinière	June 17	465	85
Ste Croix	June 18	465	87/61
St Antoine*			
St Nicolas	June 19	467	90
Returned to Quebec			
St Henry	June 24–25	468	96
Nouvelle Beauce, Ste Marie	June 26 27	469	99
Nouvelle Beauce, St Joseph	June 27	471	107
St François Seigniory	June 27	473	110

Returned to Ste Marie; Baby and Williams leave for Quebec on June 28, Taschereau on July 1; commissioners leave Quebec on July 5.

---

*The report for St Antoine is torn from the manuscript.

PARISH	DATE INSPECTED	PAGE IN FAUTEUX	PAGE IN ORIGINAL
Pointe Lévy	July 5	473	112
Beaumont	July 6	475	119
St Charles	July 6	477	123
St Michel	July 7	478	127
St Vallier	July 8	479	129
Berthier	July 8	481	134
St François du Sud	July 9	482	138
St Pierre du Sud	July 10	484	143
St Thomas	July 11	487	149
Cape St Ignace	July 11	489	153
L'Islet	July 12	491	156
St Jean Port Joli	July 12	492	159
St Roch	July 13	493	162
Ste Anne	July 13	495	166
Rivière Ouelle	July 14	498	171
Kamouraska	July 15	138	175

After leaving Kamouraska on July 16, the commissioners went to Rivière Ouelle. They spent the night of July 17 at Pointe à la Caille and then proceeded to St Michel.

Rivière des Caps to Rimousky	July 15	138	176
Kamouraska	July 16	138	177
St Michel	July 18	140	181

Notes

FOREWORD

1. "Canadians" here refers to those who then called themselves "Canadiens," that is to say, the French-speaking population of Canada. The newcomers, the British and even later the American loyalists, did not call themselves "Canadians" until they would form the majority in the 1840s.

2. Quoted by Jean-Pierre Wallot, *Un Québec qui bougeait: Trame socio-politique au tournant du XIXe siècle* (Montreal: Les Editions du Boréal Express, 1973), 256 (my translation).

3. S. D. Clark, *Movements of Political Protest in Canada, 1640–1840* (Toronto: University of Toronto Press, 1959), 93.

4. Clark, *Movements of Political Protest*, 101–4.

PREFACE TO THE CURRENT EDITION

1. Thomas Jefferson to Ebenezer Hazard, February 18, 1791, in Julian P. Boyd, ed., *The Papers of Thomas Jefferson* (Princeton, N.J.: Princeton University Press, 1974), 19:287.

2. Sir Guy Carleton (1724–1808), Lord Dorchester, served as lieutenant governor (1766–75) and then governor of Canada (1775–82, 1786–96). One of the primary architects of the Quebec Act, he successfully defended the province during the American invasion of 1775–76. Paul David Nelson, *General Sir Guy Carleton, Lord Dorchester: Soldier-Statesman of Early British Canada* (Madison, N.J.: Fairleigh Dickinson University Press, 2000); Paul R. Reynolds, *Guy Carleton: A Biography* (New York: William Morrow, 1980); Perry Eugene Leroy, "Sir Guy Carleton as a Military Leader during the American Invasion and Repulse in Canada, 1775–1776," 2 vols. (Ph.D. diss., Ohio State University, 1960).

3. The Quebec district stretched from Grondines and Deschaillons in the west to Rioux in the east. The Trois Rivières district ran from Maskinongé and Yamaska to Ste. Anne Est and Lévrard.

4. For examples of these, see Fred. C. Würtele, ed., *Blockade of Quebec in 1775–1776 by the American Revolutionists (Les Bastonnais)*, 7th ser. (Quebec: Literary and Historical Society of Quebec, 1905); Fred. C. Würtele, ed., *Blockade of Quebec in 1775–1776 by the American Revolutionists (Les Bastonnais)*, 8th ser. (Quebec: Literary and Historical Society of Quebec, 1906); John F. Roche, ed., "Quebec Under Siege, 1775–1776: The 'Memorandum' of Jacob Danford," *Canadian Historical Review* 50 (1969): 68–85; James Jeffry, "Journal Kept in Quebec in 1775 by James Jeffry," *Historical Collection of the Essex Institute* 50 (April 1914): 97–150; L'Abbé Verreau, *Invasion du Canada: Collection de Mémoires Recueillis et Annotés* (Montreal: Eusèbe Sénécal, 1873).

5. Aegidius Fauteux, *Journal de MM. Baby, Taschereau, et Williams, 1776* (Quebec, 1929).

6. Gustave Lanctôt, *Canada and the American Revolution, 1774–1783*, trans. Margaret M. Cameron (Cambridge, Mass.: Harvard University Press, 1967).

INTRODUCTION

1. General James Murray (1722–94) served as the first governor of Canada from 1764 to 1766. Francess G. Halpenny, ed., *Dictionary of Canadian Biography* (hereafter cited as *DCB*) (Toronto: University of Toronto Press, 1979), 4:569–78.

2. "The Quebec Act," in Adam Shortt and Arthur G. Doughty, eds., *Documents Relating to the Constitutional History of Canada, 1759–1791*, 2nd ed. (Ottawa: L. Taché, 1918), 1:570–76; Lanctôt, *Canada and the American Revolution*, 3–42.

3. Marc Egnal, *A Mighty Empire: The Origins of the American Revolution* (Ithaca, N.Y.: Cornell University Press, 1988), 126–49; Edmund S. Morgan and Helen M. Morgan, *The Stamp Act Crisis: Prologue to Revolution*, rev. ed. (New York: Collier Books, 1962), 48–49; Bernard Bailyn, *The Ideological Origins of the American Revolution*, rev. ed. (Cambridge, Mass.: Belknap Press, 1992), 94–145.

4. Worthington C. Ford, ed., *Journals of the Continental Congress, 1774–1789* (hereafter cited as *JCC*) (Washington, D.C.: Government Printing Office, 1905), 1:105–13.

5. *JCC*, 2:64, 67–70, 88. For an example of other such appeals, see "Philip Schuyler's Proclamation to the Inhabitants of Canada," September 5, 1775, *Papers of the Continental Congress*, microfilm ed. (hereafter cited as *PCC*) (Washington, D.C.: National Archives, 1959), M247, r172, i153, v1, p129.

6. For information on the situation in Canada in this and the next several paragraphs, see Justin H. Smith, *Our Struggle for the Fourteenth Colony: Canada and the American Revolution* (New York: Da Capo Press, 1974), 1:12–107, especially 29–40 for the peoples of Canada; Allen French, *The First Year of the American Revolution* (New York: Octagon Books, 1968), 144–47, 396–401; Christopher Ward, *The War of the Revolution* (New York: Macmillan, 1952), 1:135–39; George F. G. Stanley, *Canada Invaded, 1775–1776* (Toronto: Samuel Stevens Hakkert, 1977), 3–6; Hilda Neatby, *Quebec: The Revolutionary Age, 1760–1791* (Toronto: McClelland and Stuart, 1966), 25–141; Lanctôt, *Canada and the American Revolution*, 3–42; Alfred Leroy Burt, *The Old Province of Quebec* (Toronto: Ryerson Press, 1933), 177–201. For the Old Subjects requesting an assembly

and then petitioning for the Quebec Act's repeal, see "Letter of the Committee to Francis Maseres," November 8, 1773; "Petition to Lt. Governor for an Assembly," November 29, 1773; "Petition to the King," December 31, 1773; "Petition [to King and Parliament] for the Repeal of the Quebec Act," November 12, 1774, in Shortt and Doughty, *Constitutional History of Canada*, 1:490–91, 493–94, 495–98; 2:589–94.

7. "Journal of the Most Remarkable Occurrences in the Province of Quebec" (hereafter cited as "Ainslie Journal") in Fred C. Würtele, ed., *Blockade of Quebec in 1775–1776 by the American Revolutionists* (Les Bastonnais), 7th ser., (Quebec: Literary and Historical Society of Quebec, 1905), 12–13.

8. Stanley, *Canada Invaded*, 10; French, *First Year*, 147 n.8. For a good discussion of conflicting historiographic interpretations on whether the French Canadians accepted the Quebec Act, see George A. Rawlyk, *Revolution Rejected, 1775–1776* (Scarborough, On.: Prentice-Hall of Canada, 1968).

9. "Additional Papers concerning the Province of Quebeck," in History Section of the General Staff, ed., *A History of the Organization, Development and Services of the Military and Naval Forces of Canada from the Peace of Paris in 1763, to the Present Time* (Ottawa, 1919–20), 2:107–9; "Depositions by John Duguid and John Shatforth," August 2, 1775, *PCC*, M247, r172, i153, v1, p93; M247, r172, i153, v1, p98.

10. *JCC*, 2:109–10.

11. Michael P. Gabriel, *Major General Richard Montgomery: The Making of an American Hero* (Madison, N.J.: Fairleigh Dickinson University Press, 2002), 95–143.

12. James Kirby Martin, *Benedict Arnold, Revolutionary Hero: An American Warrior Reconsidered* (New York: New York University Press, 1997), 104–15; Kenneth Roberts, ed., *March to Quebec: Journals of the Members of Arnold's Expedition* (Garden City, N.Y.: Doubleday, Doran, 1945).

13. Roberts, *March to Quebec*, 27–40, has a full American casualty list; Guy Carleton to William Howe, January 12, 1776, in Peter Force, ed., *American Archives: Consisting of a Collection of Authentick Records, State Papers, Debates, and Letters and Other Notices of Publick Affairs, the Whole Forming a Documentary History of the Origin and Progress of the North American Colonies* (hereafter cited as *AA*) (Washington, D.C., 1839), 4:656.

14. David Wooster (1711–77), the second ranking American officer in Canada, assumed command when Montgomery was killed. Wooster arrived at Quebec on April 2 from Montreal but was succeeded by John Thomas on May 1. Wooster briefly held command again in June after Thomas died, but Congress immediately recalled him because it questioned his competence. John Thomas (1724–76) commanded American forces in Canada, arriving at Quebec on May 1. Like many of his soldiers, Thomas contracted smallpox, and he died on June 2 at Sorel. Mark Mayo Boatner III, *Encyclopedia of the American Revolution* (New York: David McKay, 1966), 1096, 1219–20.

15. James Livingston (1747–1832) was a distant relative of the influential New York Livingstons and lived near Montreal. He assisted the Americans throughout the invasion; was appointed colonel of the First Canadian Regiment on January 8, 1776; and served in the Continental army through 1781. Boatner, *Encyclopedia*, 641.

16. For examples of Canadians serving with the Americans, see James Livingston to Schuyler, September 1775, *PCC*, M247, r172, i153, v1, p162; M247, r172, i153, v1, p164; Maturin L. Delafield, ed., "Colonel Henry Beekman Livingston Letter," *Magazine of American History* 21 (January–June 1889): 258; Rudolphus Ritzema, "Journal of Colonel Rudolphus Ritzema," *Magazine of American History* 1 (February 1877): 104; Benedict Arnold to unknown, March 28, 1776, in *AA*, 5:512; Fred Anderson Berg, *Encyclopedia of Continental Army Units: Battalions, Regiments, and Independent Corps* (Harrisburg, Pa.: Stackpole Press, 1972), 16–17; Allan S. Everest, *Moses Hazen and the Canadian Refugees in the American Revolution* (Syracuse, N.Y.: Syracuse University Press, 1976).

17. Arnold to unknown, March 28, 1776, in *AA*, 5:512; Benedict Arnold to Silas Deane, March 30, 1776, in *AA*, 5:550.

18. Queen of Hungary is a reference to Maria Theresa (1717–80), the archduchess of Austria, Holy Roman Empress, and the queen of Hungary and Bohemia, who ascended to the throne in 1740. When Prussia and other powers attacked the Hapsburg Empire during the War of Austrian Succession (1740–48), Maria Theresa successfully appealed to the Hungarians to help defend her lands. She was the mother of Marie Antoinette. Edward Crankshaw, *Maria Theresa* (New York: The Viking Press, 1969).

19. W. J. Eccles, *The Canadian Frontier, 1534–1760* (Albuquerque: University of New Mexico Press, 1983), 95. The British also utilized corvée to help support their forces in Canada. See Mason Wade, *The French Canadians, 1760–1945* (Toronto: Macmillan, 1955), 73–74. Corvées could also be owed to the seigneur, in addition to the broader community. Richard Colebrook Harris, *The Seigneurial System in Early Canada: A Geographical Study* (Kingston, On.: McGill-Queen's University Press, 1984), 69–70, 71–72, 77.

20. Benedict Arnold to George Washington, November 18, 1775, in Roberts, *March to Quebec*, 84–85.

21. Stanley, *Canada Invaded*, 112; Arnold quoted in Smith, *Our Struggle*, 2:237; Benedict Arnold to Silas Deane, March 30, 1776, in *AA*, 5:550; Pierre Foretier, "Notes and Reminiscences of an Inhabitant of Montreal during the Occupation of That City by the Bostonians from 1775 to 1776," in *Canada Public Records Report, 1945* (Ottawa: Edmund Cloutier, 1946), xxv–xxvi; Richard Montgomery to Schuyler, December 26, 1775, *PCC*, M247, r189, i170, v2, p247; Ritzema, "Journal," 106.

22. History Section of the General Staff, *Military and Naval Forces of Canada*, 2:89.

23. Quoted in "Ainslie Journal," 54, 69 (quote).

24. Smith, *Our Struggle*, 2:233–34; Stanley, *Canada Invaded*, 110–18; Lanctôt, *Canada and the American Revolution*, 110; Scott McDermott, *Charles Carroll of Carrollton: Faithful Revolutionary* (New York: Scepter, 2002), 129–38; Gayle K. Brown, "The Impact of the Colonial Anti-Catholic Tradition on the Canadian Campaign, 1775–1776," *Journal of Church and State* 35 (Summer 1993): 559–75.

25. Arnold to Deane, March 30, 1776, in *AA*, 5:550.

26. Foretier, "Notes and Reminiscences," xxiii–xxiv; "Ainslie Journal," 83; "Journal of the

Siege From the 1st. Dec., 1775," in Würtele, *Blockade of Quebec* (1906), 99; Roche, "Danford Memorandum," 85.

27. John Sullivan (1740–95) saw extensive service throughout the Revolutionary War, most notably leading a punitive raid against the Iroquois in New York from May to November 1779. Charles P. Whittemore, *A General of the Revolution: John Sullivan of New Hampshire* (New York: Columbia University Press, 1961).

28. William Thompson (1736–81) commanded a battalion of Pennsylvania riflemen. Captured at Trois Rivières, he was soon paroled but not officially exchanged for four years. Boatner, *Encyclopedia*, 1098–99.

29. Ward, *War of Revolution*, 1:198–200; Paul David Nelson, *Anthony Wayne: Soldier of the Republic* (Bloomington: Indiana University Press, 1985), 24–26.

30. Lanctôt, *Canada and the American Revolution*, 141–45; Stanley, *Canada Invaded*, 119–23, 126–33.

31. Carleton also established a commission in the Montreal district headed by Adam Mabane, Thomas Dunn, and Pierre Panet, but its report is not extant. See Lanctôt, *Canada and the American Revolution*, 152.

32. Frederick Haldimand (1718–91), a Swiss mercenary in the British army, saw extensive service in America during the Seven Years' War. He served as governor of Canada from 1778 to 1784. Boatner, *Encyclopedia*, 474–75.

33. *DCB*, 5:41–46.

34. *DCB*, 5:793–95.

35. *DCB*, 5:862–65.

36. Eleven parish reports do not record how many men attended the muster.

37. The parishes and number of men barred from service are as follows: Vieille Lorette, 3; L'Ange Gardien, 1; St. Jean—Ile D'Orléans, 2; St. Pierre—Ile D'Orléans, 3; Ste. Anne, 6; Batiscan, 5; Gentilly, 5; St. Pierre des Becquets, 9; Lotbinière, 2; St. Nichols, 1; Pointe Lévy, 3; St. Pierre du Sud, 9; St. Thomas, 6; Ste. Anne, 7.

38. R. Arthur Bowler, *Logistics and the Failure of the British Army in America, 1775–1783* (Princeton, N.J.: Princeton University Press, 1975), 212–22; R. Arthur Bowler, "Sir Guy Carleton and the Campaign of 1776 in Canada" *Canadian Historical Review* 55 (June 1974): 134–37.

JOURNAL

1. The priests' full names are found in Marcel Trudel, *L'Église Canadienne sous le Régime Militaire, 1759–1764: I Les Problèmes* (Ottawa: Les Études de L'Institut d'Histoire de L'Amérique Française, 1956), 348–57, unless otherwise noted.

2. In the British system, a bailiff was a local magistrate who had authority to serve writs and make arrests.

3. Established in 1693 and located near the St. Charles River on the edge of the suburb of St. Roch, the General Hospital was operated by nuns. American troops used the hos-

· pital throughout the siege. George Heriot, *Travels through the Canadas Containing a Description of the Picturesque Scenery on Some of the Rivers and Lakes; With an Account of the Productions, Commerce, and Inhabitants of Those Provinces* (Rutland, Vt.: Charles E. Tuttle, 1971), 71–72; Smith, *Our Struggle*, 2:98–99, 148–49.

4. "King's woods" is probably a reference to the white pine (*Pinus strobus*) and other wood used for shipbuilding. Robert Greenhalgh Albion, *Forests and Sea Power: The Timber Problem of the Royal Navy, 1652–1862* (Hamden, Conn.: Archon Books, 1965), 31, 232. For Canadian lumber and shipbuilding, see W. J. Eccles, *France in America* (New York: Harper and Row, 1973), 82–83, 123; Paul Walden Bamford, *Forests and French Sea Power, 1660–1789* (Toronto: University of Toronto Press, 1956), 114–28; Heriot, *Travels*, 63, 73. Hector Theophilus Cramahé (1720–88) held a wide array of offices in Quebec during his career, including civil secretary to three governors, judge of the Court of Common Pleas, and lieutenant governor from 1771 to 1782. A former British officer, Cramahé prepared Quebec for siege in fall 1775 while Carleton was in Montreal trying to repel the American invasion. *DCB*, 4:787–93.

5. The original manuscript repeatedly records salaries in livres, the official monetary unit in New France, whose symbol is similar to #, except it only has one horizontal bar. This translation will use # for livre. The version published by the Archives of Quebec used "lb." For a discussion on a livre's value and its symbol, see Joseph L. Peyser, ed. and trans., *On the Eve of the Conquest: The Chevalier de Raymond's Critique of New France in 1754* (East Lansing: Michigan State University Press, 1997), 34 n4.

6. The unsuccessful American attack on Quebec.

7. Pierre-Régnier de Roussi (d. 1810) was a French Canadian who assisted the Americans both during the invasion and later in the Revolutionary War. In November 1775, Montgomery commissioned him as a lieutenant colonel in the militia, and Arnold gave him the same rank in the First Canadian Regiment in January 1776. De Roussi accompanied the Americans when they retreated from the province and served as an officer in several different regiments until he resigned his commission in 1780. Philander D. Chase, ed., *The Papers of George Washington: Revolutionary War Series* (Charlottesville: University Press of Virginia, 1997), 7:178 n2. Jean Garneau owned one of the subfiefs belonging to Antoine Juchereau Duchesnay. See *DCB*, 5:463. Also see note 74.

8. *DCB*, 3:227.

9. Named after a Franciscan monastery built in 1694 on a rocky point near the St. Lawrence River. British forces destroyed the monastery during the 1759 siege of Quebec, and its ruins were still visible as late as 1806. Heriot, *Travels*, 94.

10. Jean-François Hubert (1739–97) was a director and bursar of the Quebec Seminary. In 1786, he became coadjutor bishop of Quebec and bishop in 1788. *DCB*, 4:370–75.

11. Probably the Falls of the Montmorency, approximately six miles from Quebec. *Lovell's Gazetteer of British North America, 1873* (Milton, On.: Global Heritage Press, 1999), 422.

12. Lesperance was such a staunch American partisan that his priest, Father Corbin, ordered him to hold a candle symbolizing repentance when he publicly renounced the

rebels' cause in spring 1776. Lanctôt, *Canada and the American Revolution*, 161.

13. Henri-François Gravé de la Rive (1730–1802) served as the superior and bursar of the Quebec Seminary. *DCB*, 5:379–80.

14. "*Bostonnais*" is a reference to Bostonians. The French Canadians often called the Americans "*Les Bostonnais*" whether they were from Massachusetts or not. Sometimes spelled "*Bastonnais*," this probably reflects how New Englanders pronounced it with their accent. See David Hackett Fischer, *Paul Revere's Ride* (New York: Oxford University Press, 1994), 4–5.

15. Louis-Liénard de Beaujeu de Villemomble (1716–1802) was a former French colonial officer and one-time commander of Michilimackinac. In 1776, he was the seigneur of Ile aux Grues, where he resided. British authorities requested that he raise a loyalist detachment to attack the American post at Pointe Lévy. The Americans discovered and routed his advance guard on March 25, 1776, at Michel Blay's house in St. Pierre du Sud. *DCB*, 3:402–3; 4:72, 639.

16. A piastre was a coin similar to a Spanish piece of eight.

17. Jeremiah (John) Duggan, a grain dealer near Sorel and a former Quebec barber, actively assisted the Americans during the invasion. He participated in Ethan Allen's failed September 25, 1775, attempt to seize Montreal; was present when the Americans captured Fort Chambly; and later helped recruit Canadian troops. Smith, *Our Struggle*, 1:389, 401, 402, 405, 426; 2:221–22; History Section of the General Staff, *Military and Naval Forces of Canada*, 2:5–6, 77–78.

18. Carleton tried to mobilize the Canadian militia and had some success, especially after Ethan Allen's defeat at Montreal on September 25, 1775. By mid-October, approximately twelve hundred militia had gathered at Montreal from outlying areas, but the governor failed to use them aggressively to break Montgomery's siege of St. Jeans. In the face of this inactivity and Chambly's surrender on October 18, some militia began to drift away. On October 30, Carleton attacked the Americans at Longueuil with approximately one thousand Canadians, Indians, and regulars but was repelled. St. Jeans surrendered on November 3, and the Canadian militia began to desert in greater numbers. Lanctôt, *Canada and the American Revolution*, 83–89; Stanley, *Canada Invaded*, 46–49, 56–60. See note 46 for additional information on Allen.

19. François Le Guerne (1725–89) was ordained in Paris in 1751 and then assigned to Acadia. Following the British conquest of the region in 1755, he organized approximately two hundred families in resisting deportation. Fearing arrest, Le Guerne fled Acadia to Quebec and was assigned to St. François. *DCB*, 4:452–53.

20. *DCB*, 5:51. Louis-Philippe Mariauchau D'Esgly (1710–88) was the first Canadian-born bishop. In 1772, Bishop Jean-Olivier Briand made him his coadjutor, but he continued to minister to the people of Ile d'Orléans. He became bishop of Quebec when Briand resigned in 1784 and held the position until his death. *DCB*, 4:510–12.

21. Possibly near present-day Ste. Pétronille, near the tip of Ile d'Orléans.

22. Adam Mabane (ca. 1734–92), a physician by training, was a judge of the Court of Common Pleas. In 1775, Carleton appointed him to Quebec's Legislative Council.

DCB, 4:491–94. William Grant (1744–1805) was a wealthy merchant and seigneur from St. Roch who strongly supported the British during the American invasion. Many of his buildings, including his house, were destroyed during the siege of Quebec. *DCB*, 5:367–76. Nicolas-Gaspard Boisseau (1726–1804) was the chief clerk of the provost court of Quebec. *DCB*, 4:75–76, 692.

23. Jean-Baptiste Le Comte Dupré (1731–1820) was a wealthy merchant who served as a major in the Quebec militia. *DCB*, 5:481–82.

24. Cap Rouge is a small village southwest of Ste. Foye, near the mouth of the river of the same name. The cape itself is named after the reddish slate visible on a bluff overlooking the St. Lawrence. Heriot, *Travels*, 98–99.

25. See introduction for a discussion of fascines.

26. Father Lotbinière's younger brother, François-Louis Chartier de Lotbinière (1716–ca. 1785), was a defrocked Récollet priest who served as a chaplain to pro-American Canadians during the campaign. *DCB*, 4:141–43.

27. Maurice Desdevens de Glandons (1742–99), a surveyor, strongly supported the American effort in Canada. He helped transport American weapons and supplies to Quebec in early December 1775 and stopped deserters from escaping up the St. Lawrence toward Montreal. Following the American defeat on December 31, Desdevens helped recruit troops to support the American army. He left the province in 1776 with the retreating Americans and resided in the United States for ten years before returning to Canada. [John] Macpherson (for Richard Montgomery) to Maurice Desdevens, December 1, 1775; Macpherson (for Montgomery) to Maurice Desdevens, December 30, 1775, *PCC*, M247, r41, i35, 219; *DCB*, 4:215–16; "Papers Belonging to L'Anglais of the Ecureuils"; "General David Wooster to All Captains of Militia," January 6, 1776; "Extract of a Letter Addressed to Maurice Desdevens," in History Section of the General Staff, *Military and Naval Forces of Canada*, 2:89–90, 139–40, 141–42.

28. The *Gaspé* was one of eleven vessels that the Americans captured near the mouth of the Richelieu River on November 19, 1775, as Carleton evacuated Montreal. Montgomery then used the *Gaspé* and another ship, the *Mary*, to transport three hundred soldiers from Montreal to Point aux Tremble, where he met Arnold's command on December 1, 1775. Gabriel, *Major General Richard Montgomery*, 138–39, 142–43.

29. More commonly known as the Richelieu or Sorel, the river flows northward from Lake Champlain and enters the St. Lawrence at the town of Sorel.

30. Louis-Joseph Godefroy de Tonnancour (1712–84) was a wealthy merchant and seigneur who served as the king's attorney and keeper of stores. Tonnancour was the militia colonel of Trois Rivières and supported the British during the invasion. *DCB*, 4:304–5.

31. Allan Maclean (1725–98), a British officer, raised the First Battalion of the Royal Highland Emigrants Regiment to help resist the American invasion. He assisted Carleton in an unsuccessful attempt to relieve St. Jeans in late October 1775, advancing to Sorel. He then retreated to Quebec, helped organize its defenses, and participated in repulsing the December 31 American assault on the town. *DCB*, 4:503–4.

32. Langlois assisted the American effort to organize a provincial convention to select Canadian delegates to attend the Continental Congress in Philadelphia. He also helped enlist troops for them. "Papers Belonging to L'Anglais of the Ecureuils"; "Extract of a Letter Addressed to Maurice Desdevens," in History Section of the General Staff, *Military and Naval Forces of Canada*, 2:89–90, 141–42.

33. An écu equaled three livres. Peyser, *Eve of Conquest*, 133 n67.

34. St. Jeans, a British fort on the Richelieu River, fell to Montgomery's forces after a siege lasting from September 17 to November 3, 1775. Gabriel, *Major General Richard Montgomery*, 105–29.

35. Littlejohn was captain of the *Charlotta*, one of the ships anchored near Quebec during the siege. Littlejohn commanded a company of British sailors that served in the garrison. *Quebec Gazette*, October 5, 1775; Allex Harrow to Thomas Forsyth, August 20, 1800, in History Section of the General Staff, *Military and Naval Forces of Canada*, 2:85, 136.

36. The Americans began digging entrenchments near Deschambault, a natural strong-point on the St. Lawrence, in spring 1776, just as the French had during the Seven Years' War. The town, located on high ground, overlooked a narrow channel in the river that was difficult for ships to pass. While retreating from Quebec, the American army halted at Deschambault from May 7 to 13 but then resumed its retreat to Sorel. Smith, *Our Struggle*, 2:303–9, 323–24, 343–49.

37. In addition to serving as the militia captain, Louis Gouin also managed Charles-Louis Tarieu de Lanaudière's lands near Ste. Anne. *DCB*, 5:792.

38. William Goforth (1731–1807), a captain in the First New York Regiment, commanded the American troops at Trois Rivières. "Gershom Mott to Captain Goforth," March 26, 1776, in *AA*, 5:753; Chase, *Papers of George Washington*, 4:319 n1.

39. *DCB*, 4:439; 5:164.

40. Charles-Louis Tarieu de Lanaudière (1743–1811), the son of Charles-François Tarieu de La Naudière, was a member of the French Canadian seigneurial and military elite. He attached himself to the British authorities and served as Carleton's aide-de-camp. Lanaudière helped rally militia to repel the American invasion in 1775. He was with Carleton when the British governor escaped from the Americans near the mouth of the Richelieu River in November 1775. *DCB*, 5:791–92. Also see note 68.

41. Etienne Montgolfier (1712–91) arrived in Canada in 1751 and eventually became the superior of the Sulpician Order in Montreal. Governor James Murray appointed him vicar general in 1766, and Montgolfier strongly supported the British during the American invasion. At Bishop Jean-Olivier Briand's request, Montgolfier issued sermons to priests in the Montreal district urging parishioners to remain loyal to Britain. *DCB*, 4:542–45.

Jean-Olivier Briand (1715–94) was appointed the Roman Catholic bishop of Quebec in 1766 and served until 1784. Briand steadfastly supported the British during the invasion by issuing a proclamation encouraging loyalty to the crown. He also instructed his priests to withhold the sacraments from Canadians who sided with the rebellion. *DCB*, 4:94–103; Lanctôt, *Canada and the American Revolution*, 50–56, 85–86.

42. Pierre Garreau *dit* Saint-Onge (1722–95), a close friend of Bishop Briand, was named vicar general of Trois Rivières in 1764 yet continued to minister to individual parishes. During the American invasion, Father Garreau strongly sided with the British by holding public prayers and novenas for them. Many of his parishioners resented this, however, because they favored the Americans. *DCB*, 4:287–88.

43. Fleuve refers to the St. Lawrence River.

44. St. Paul Lake, located in Nicolet County, Quebec, is five miles long and empties into the St. Lawrence via the Godefroi River. *Lovell's Gazetteer*, 448.

45. Arnold's troops did not cross the St. Lawrence to Quebec until the night of November 15. He subsequently withdrew to Pointe aux Trembles to await Montgomery. The combined American force did not return to Quebec until December 4. Stanley, *Canada Invaded*, 78–81, 87.

46. Ethan Allen (1738–89) was one of the leaders of the Green Mountain Boys. He won notoriety by capturing Fort Ticonderoga with Benedict Arnold on May 10, 1775, and served as a volunteer during the American invasion. Allen enlisted Canadians to fight for the invaders. On September 25, he led an unsuccessful attack on Montreal, during which he was captured. Michael A. Bellesiles, *Revolutionary Outlaws: Ethan Allen and the Struggle for Independence on the Early American Frontier* (Charlottesville: University Press of Virginia, 1993).

47. Probably Richard Montgomery's aide, John Macpherson, who was killed with the general on December 31.

48. Ecuyer, a British half-pay officer, helped organize an English militia in Quebec in July 1775. Although his full identity is unknown, he may have been Simeon Ecuyer (1720–?), a Swiss-born mercenary who served in the Royal American Regiment (Sixtieth Regiment) during the Seven Years' War and commanded Fort Pitt during Pontiac's uprising in 1763–64. Jeffry, "Journal," 122; Henry Bouquet, *Papers of Henry Bouquet* (Harrisburg: Pennsylvania Historical and Museum Commission, 1994), 6:84 n4.

49. As Montgomery's troops approached Montreal in November 1775, Carleton and the city's garrison retreated down the St. Lawrence in eleven vessels. Montgomery had sent troops to the mouth of the Richelieu River to cut off the British retreat, and they captured the flotilla on November 19, but not before Carleton escaped in a canoe. Richard Montgomery to Schuyler, November 17, 1775, Schuyler Papers; Richard Montgomery to unknown [Bedel?], November 16, 1775, in W. T. R. Saffell, ed., *Records of the Revolutionary War: Containing the Military and Financial Correspondence of Distinguished Officers*, 3rd ed. (Baltimore: Charles C. Saffell, 1894), 27–28; Harry Parker Ward, ed., "Diary of Captain John Fassett, Jr.," in *The Follett-Dewey Fassett-Safford Ancestry of Captain Martin Dewey Follett* (Columbus, Ohio: Champlin, 1896), 235; Ritzema, "Journal," 103; Brown to Richard Montgomery, November 7, 1775, *PCC*, M247, r179, i161, p397; Return of Military Supplies, Ordinance, Troops, & c on Board the Vessels, November 19, 1775, in *AA*, 3:1693–94.

50. On November 25, the frigate *Hunter*, the brig *Fell*, and two small schooners arrived off Pointe aux Trembles. Arnold correctly guessed that they were sailing for Cap Santé to

intercept Montgomery. Two days later, Arnold sent forty men to escort Montgomery's command, which was falsely rumored to be approaching. This detachment is probably the one that went with Pagé, but it is unlikely that the American sent much ammunition to the *habitants*, because he had little to spare. The British ships did not find Montgomery's flotilla and returned to Quebec on November 30. Roberts, *March to Quebec*, 96–100.

51. The Falls of the Chaudière, four miles from the river's mouth, are approximately one hundred feet high.

52. Beauce is the region along the Chaudière River to the Maine border.

53. A sou is a coin of little value.

54. The preceding paragraphs seem to describe three separate, but similar, incidents of Americans or their Canadian allies arresting loyalists.

55. *DCB*, 4:8, 43.

56. Michel Blay (ca. 1711–83), the militia captain and coseigneur at St. Pierre, remained loyal to the British during the invasion. Beaujeu's loyalist advance guard encamped at his house, where it was routed on March 25, 1776, by the Americans and some of their Canadian allies. Seven loyalists were killed, two wounded, and thirty-eight taken prisoners. The Americans had six dead and a number wounded. *DCB*, 4:71–72.

57. The area along the St. Lawrence below Quebec, such as Kamouraska and Rivière Ouelle.

58. The St. John River, the largest in New Brunswick, has its headwaters in the mountains along the Maine-Quebec border. *Lovell's Gazetteer*, 445.

59. Arnold arrived at Ste. Marie on November 4 and was well received by the *habitants*, who sold his starving troops provisions as they straggled into the village over the next few days. Martin, *Arnold*, 140–42; Roberts, *March to Quebec*, 140–41, 220–22.

60. The Rivière du Sud flows into the St. Lawrence below Quebec near St. Thomas. *Lovell's Gazetteer*, 455.

61. A beadle was a minor parish official who helped maintain order. They sometimes had a civil function as well.

62. Probably Thomas Dunn (1729–1818), a wealthy English merchant who served as a judge on the Court of Common Pleas for Quebec and Trois Rivières. Dunn was also a member of Carleton's privy council. *DCB*, 5:287–93.

63. Joseph de Fleury de La Gorgendière (1676–1755) was the seigneur of Deschambault and St. François in Nouvelle Beauce. He was Gabriel Taschereau's grandfather. *DCB*, 3:216–18.

64. *DCB*, 4:142.

65. Pointe à la Caille, near St. Thomas, is where the Rivière à la Caille flows into the St. Lawrence. *Lovell's Gazetteer*, 378.

66. Alexander Fraser (1729–99), a former British officer, was the seigneur of La Martinière and Vitre near Quebec. He served as an officer in Maclean's Royal Highland Emigrants Regiment during the invasion. *DCB*, 4:276.

67. Clément Gosselin (1747–1816) was one of the most active pro-American partisans in

Canada. Some of his activities included recruiting troops for the invaders, organizing parish elections to select new officers, and participating in the attack on Beaujeu's force at Michel Blay's house. He also may have been at the unsuccessful American assault on Quebec on December 31, 1775. On March 4, 1776, he became a captain in Moses Hazen's American Second Canadian Regiment. When the invaders retreated in spring 1776, Gosselin went into hiding for a period but was arrested in 1777. Following his 1778 release, he rejoined his regiment but returned to Canada on spying missions a number of times. He later fought in the Yorktown campaign of 1781, where he was wounded. *DCB*, 5:358–59.

68. Marie-Catherine Le Moyne de Longueuil was the widow of Charles-François Tarieu de La Naudière (1710–76), the seigneur of St. Vallier, St. Pierre des Becquets, and Lac-Maskinonge. La Naudière briefly served on Quebec's Legislative Council but died on February 1, 1776. *DCB*, 4:728–30.

69. James Cuthbert, a former British officer and the seigneur of Berthier, called upon the *habitants* to serve, claiming that it was their obligation to do so. The *habitants* ignored his order and threatened to pillage the property of anyone who enlisted. *DCB*, 4:190–91; "Additional Papers Concerning the Province of Quebeck," in History Section of the General Staff, *Military and Naval Forces of Canada*, 2:108–9.

70. The Cove of Bellechasse lies between St. Vallier and Berthier, where the Bellechasse and Meres rivers enter the St. Lawrence.

71. Donald MacKinnon (McKinnon) was a lieutenant in Maclean's Royal Highland Emigrants Regiment. Stanley, *Canada Invaded*, 155.

72. *DCB*, 5:736. Charles-François Bailly de Messein (1740–94) was one of Carleton's trusted friends and tutored his children. In March 1776, he served as the chaplain for the loyalists that Louis Liénard de Beaujeu de Villemomble raised on the south bank of the St. Lawrence. Bailly was shot in the stomach and captured when the Americans routed Beaujeu's advanced guard at St. Pierre du Sud on March 25, 1776. Bailly survived his wounds and was eventually released. In 1788, he was named coadjutor bishop of Quebec. *DCB*, 4:41–44.

73. Jean-Baptiste Lebrun de Duplessis (ca. 1739–1807) was a French soldier who deserted to join the British in 1760. Following the British conquest of Canada, Lebrun became a lawyer and notary in Quebec. Carleton revoked these commissions in 1769, however, because of misconduct. *DCB*, 5:478–80.

74. Antoine Juchereau Duchesnay (1740–1806), Louis Liénard de Beaujeu de Villemomble's son-in-law, was the seigneur of Beauport, Fossembault, Gaudarville, and St. Roch-des-Aulnaies. One of the many seigneurs who actively fought against the Americans during the invasion, Duchesnay became a prisoner of war when St. Jeans fell to Montgomery's forces on November 3, 1775. He was held for eighteen months before being released and returned to Canada. *DCB*, 5:462–64.

75. *Habitants* stood guard to protect their parishes from British forces and to prevent supplies being delivered to Quebec. See the reports from Ile D'Orléans–St. Laurent, St.

Pierre des Becquets, Pointe Lévy, St. Michel, St. Vallier, Berthier, and St. Thomas for examples.

76. Pierre-Antoine Porlier (1725–89) firmly opposed the American invasion and encouraged his parishioners to join Beaujeu's loyalist forces. Father Porlier also wrote Bishop Briand a detailed account of his parishioners' behavior during the invasion. *DCB*, 4:638–39.

77. William Ross, a veteran of the Seventy-eighth Regiment, Fraser's Highlanders, became a merchant after the British conquest. He helped organize Beaujeu's force in March 1776. History Section of the General Staff, *Military and Naval Forces of Canada*, 2:22.

78. Mille Vaches, a small village on the north bank of the St. Lawrence, lies between Rivière du Sault au Mouton and Rivière Porteneuf in Saguenay County. *Lovell's Gazetteer*, 195.

79. *DCB*, 3:560.

80. The skirmish at St. Pierre du Sud where the Americans and pro-American *habitants* dispersed Beaujeu's advance guard at Michel Blay's house.

81. Pointe de la Rivière du Loup.

82. Rivière des Caps lies between Kamouraska and Rivière du Loup, near the Pilgrim Islands.

Bibliography

Primary Sources

MANUSCRIPT COLLECTIONS

Papers of the Continental Congress. microfilm ed., 204 reels. Washington, D.C.: National Archives, 1959.

University of Montreal, Archives Division, Baby, Taschereau, and Williams Journal; p58, Collection Louis-François-George Baby, 1832–1906.

PRINTED PRIMARY SOURCES

Bouquet, Henry. *The Papers of Henry Bouquet.* 6 vols. Harrisburg: Pennsylvania Historical and Museum Commission, 1972–94.

Boyd, Julian P., ed. *The Papers of Thomas Jefferson.* 31 vols. Princeton, N.J.: Princeton University Press, 1950–2004.

Chase, Philander D., ed. *The Papers of George Washington: Revolutionary War Series.* 10 vols. Charlottesville: University Press of Virginia, 1985–2000.

Delafield, Maturin L., ed. "Colonel Henry Beekman Livingston Letter." *Magazine of American History* 21 (January–June 1889): 256–58.

Fauteux, Aegidius, ed. *Journal de MM. Baby, Taschereau, et Williams, 1776.* Quebec, 1929.

———. "Journal par Messrs Frans Baby, Gab. Taschereau et Jenkin Williams dans la Tournée qu'ils ont fait dans le District de Québec. . . ." *Rapport de L'Archiviste de la Province de Québec* (1927–28): 435–99; (1929–30): 138–40.

Force, Peter, ed. *American Archives: Consisting of a Collection of Authentick Records, State Papers, Debates, and Letters and Other Notices of Publick Affairs, the Whole Forming a Documentary History of the Origin and Progress of the North American Colonies.* 9 vols. Washington, D.C., 1837–53.

Ford, Worthington C., ed. *Journals of the Continental Congress, 1774–1789.* 34 vols. Washington, D.C.: Government Printing Office, 1904–37.

Foretier, Pierre. "Notes and Reminiscences of an Inhabitant of Montreal during the Occupation of That City by the Bostonians from 1775 to 1776." *Canada Public Records Report,*

1945. Ottawa: Edmund Cloutier, 1946.

Heriot, George. *Travels through the Canadas Containing a Description of the Picturesque Scenery on Some of the Rivers and Lakes; With an Account of the Productions, Commerce, and Inhabitants of Those Provinces.* Rutland, Vt.: Charles E. Tuttle, 1971.

History Section of the General Staff, ed. *A History of the Organization, Development and Services of the Military and Naval Forces of Canada from the Peace of Paris in 1763, to the Present Time.* 3 vols. Ottawa, 1919–20.

Jeffry, James. "Journal Kept in Quebec in 1775 by James Jeffry." *Historical Collection of the Essex Institute,* 50 (April 1914): 97–150.

Peyser, Joseph L., ed. and trans. *On the Eve of the Conquest: The Chevalier de Raymond's Critique of New France in 1754.* East Lansing: Michigan State University Press, 1997.

Ritzema, Rudolphus. "Journal of Colonel Rudolphus Ritzema." *Magazine of American History* 1 (February 1877): 98–107.

Roberts, Kenneth, ed. *March to Quebec: Journals of the Members of Arnold's Expedition.* Garden City, N.Y.: Doubleday, Doran, 1945.

Roche, John F., ed. "Quebec Under Siege, 1775–1776: The 'Memorandum' of Jacob Danford." *Canadian Historical Review* 50 (1969): 68–85.

Saffell, W. T. R., ed. *Records of the Revolutionary War: Containing the Military and Financial Correspondence of Distinguished Officers.* 3rd ed. Baltimore: Charles C. Saffell, 1894.

Shortt, Adam, and Arthur G. Doughty, eds. *Documents Relating to the Constitutional History of Canada, 1759–1791.* 2 vols., 2nd ed. Ottawa: L. Taché, 1918.

Verreau, L'Abbé. *Invasion du Canada: Collection de Mémoires Recueillis et Annotés* (Montreal: Eusèbe Sénécal, 1873).

Ward, Harry Parker, ed. "Diary of Captain John Fassett, Jr." In *The Follett-Dewey Fassett-Safford Ancestry of Captain Martin Dewey Follett.* Columbus, Ohio: Champlin Printing, 1896.

Würtele, Fred. C., ed. *Blockade of Quebec in 1775–1776 by the American Revolutionists (Les Bastonnais).* 7th ser. Quebec: Literary and Historical Society of Quebec, 1905.

———. *Blockade of Quebec in 1775–1776 by the American Revolutionists (Les Bastonnais).* 8th ser. Quebec: Literary and Historical Society of Quebec, 1906.

Secondary Sources

Albion, Robert Greenhalgh. *Forests and Sea Power: The Timber Problem of the Royal Navy, 1652–1862.* Hamden, Conn.: Archon Books, 1965.

Bailyn, Bernard. *The Ideological Origins of the American Revolution.* Rev. ed. Cambridge, Mass.: Belknap Press, 1992.

Bamford, Paul Walden. *Forests and French Sea Power, 1660–1789.* Toronto: University of Toronto Press, 1956.

Bellesiles, Michael A. *Revolutionary Outlaws: Ethan Allen and the Struggle for Independence on the Early American Frontier.* Charlottesville: University Press of Virginia, 1993.

Berg, Fred Anderson. *Encyclopedia of Continental Army Units: Battalions, Regiments, and Independent Corps.* Harrisburg, Pa.: Stackpole Press, 1972.

Boatner, Mark Mayo, III. *Encyclopedia of the American Revolution.* New York: David McKay, 1966.

Bowler, R. Arthur. *Logistics and the Failure of the British Army in America, 1775–1783.* Princeton, N.J.: Princeton University Press, 1975.

———. "Sir Guy Carleton and the Campaign of 1776 in Canada." *Canadian Historical Review* 55 (June 1974): 131–40.

Brown, Gayle K. "The Impact of the Colonial Anti-Catholic Tradition on the Canadian Campaign, 1775–1776." *Journal of Church and State* 35 (Summer 1993): 559–75.

Burt, Alfred Leroy. *The Old Province of Quebec.* Toronto: Ryerson Press, 1933.

Clark, S. D. *Movements of Political Protest in Canada, 1640–1840.* Toronto: University of Toronto Press, 1959.

Crankshaw, Edward. *Maria Theresa.* New York: The Viking Press, 1969.

Eccles, W. J. *The Canadian Frontier, 1534–1760.* Albuquerque: University of New Mexico Press, 1983.

———. *France in America.* New York: Harper and Row, 1973.

Egnal, Marc. *A Mighty Empire: The Origins of the American Revolution.* Ithaca, N.Y.: Cornell University Press, 1988.

Everest, Allan S. *Moses Hazen and the Canadian Refugees in the American Revolution.* Syracuse, N.Y.: Syracuse University Press, 1976.

Fischer, David Hackett. *Paul Revere's Ride.* New York: Oxford University Press, 1994.

French, Allen. *The First Year of the American Revolution.* New York: Octagon Books, 1968.

Gabriel, Michael P. *Major General Richard Montgomery: The Making of an American Hero.* Madison, N.J.: Fairleigh Dickinson University Press, 2002.

Haarman, Albert W., and Donald W. Holst. "The Friedrich von Germann Drawings of Troops in the American Revolution." *Military Collector and Historian* 16 (Spring 1964): 1–9.

Halpenny, Francess G., ed. *Dictionary of Canadian Biography.* 14 vols. Toronto: University of Toronto Press, 1966–94.

Harris, R. Cole, ed. *Historical Atlas of Canada.* Vol. 1, *From the Beginning to 1800.* Toronto: University of Toronto Press, 1987.

Harris, Richard Colebrook. *The Seigneurial System in Early Canada: A Geographical Study.* Kingston, On.: McGill-Queen's University Press, 1984.

Lanctôt, Gustave. *Canada and the American Revolution, 1774–1783.* Trans. Margaret M. Cameron. Cambridge, Mass.: Harvard University Press, 1967.

Leroy, Perry Eugene. "Sir Guy Carleton as a Military Leader during the American Invasion and Repulse in Canada, 1775–1776." 2 vols. Ph.D. diss., Ohio State University, 1960.

Lovell's Gazetteer of British North America, 1873. Milton, On.: Global Heritage Press, 1999.

Martin, James Kirby. *Benedict Arnold, Revolutionary Hero: An American Warrior Reconsidered.* New York: New York University Press, 1997.

McDermott, Scott. *Charles Carroll of Carrollton: Faithful Revolutionary.* New York: Scepter, 2002.

Morgan, Edmund S., and Helen M. Morgan. *The Stamp Act Crisis: Prologue to Revolution.* Rev. ed. New York: Collier Books, 1962.

Neatby, Hilda. *Quebec: The Revolutionary Age, 1760–1791.* Toronto: McClelland and Stuart, 1966.

Nelson, Paul David. *Anthony Wayne: Soldier of the Republic.* Bloomington: Indiana University Press, 1985.

———. *General Sir Guy Carleton, Lord Dorchester: Soldier-Statesman of Early British Canada.* Madison, N.J.: Fairleigh Dickinson University Press, 2000.

Noël, Françoise. *The Christie Seigneuries: Estate Management and Settlement in the Upper Richelieu Valley, 1760–1854.* Kingston, On.: McGill-Queen's University Press, 1992.

Park, Edwards. "Could Canada Have Ever Been Our Fourteenth Colony?" *Smithsonian* 18 (December 1987): 41–49.

Pearson, Michael. "The Siege of Quebec, 1775–1776: A Colony Preserved." *American Heritage* 23 (February 1972): 8–15, 104–8.

Rawlyk, George A. *Revolution Rejected, 1775–1776.* Scarborough, On.: Prentice-Hall of Canada, 1968.

Reynolds, Paul R. *Guy Carleton: A Biography.* New York: William Morrow, 1980.

Smith, Justin H. *Our Struggle for the Fourteenth Colony: Canada and the American Revolution.* 2 vols. New York: Da Capo Press, 1974.

Stanley, George F. G. *Canada Invaded, 1775–1776.* Toronto: Samuel Stevens Hakkert, 1977.

Stevens, Michael E., and Steven B. Burg. *Editing Historical Documents: A Handbook of Practice.* Walnut Creek, Calif.: AltaMira Press, 1997.

Trudel, Marcel. *L'Église Canadienne sous le Régime Militaire, 1759–1764: I Les Problèmes.* Ottawa: Les Études de L'Institut d'Histoire de L'Amérique Française, 1956.

Wade, Mason. *French Canadians, 1760–1945.* New York: Macmillan, 1955.

Wallot, Jean-Pierre. *Un Québec qui bougeait: Trame socio-politique au tournant du XIXe siècle.* Montreal: Les Editions du Boréal Express, 1973.

Ward, Christopher. *The War of the Revolution.* 2 vols. New York: Macmillan, 1952.

Whittemore, Charles P. *A General of the Revolution: John Sullivan of New Hampshire.* New York: Columbia University Press, 1961.

Index

Ecuyer, (Simeon?), 51, 131

Elections and assemblies, parish: to recruit, 95, 99, 107, 110; to select officers, 32, 38–40, 45, 66, 77, 83, 85, 95, 97, 99–100

First Continental Congress, xvi; meets, xxxi; sends appeal to Canadians, xiii–xiv

Fleury de la Gorgendière, Joseph de, 64, 132

Franklin, Benjamin, xiv–xvi

Fraser, Alexander, 72, 132

Garreau, *dit* Saint-Onge, Pierre, 42, 131

Godefroy de Tonnancour, Louis-Joseph, 27, 129

Goforth, William, 130

Gosselin, Clément, xxxvi, 106–7; appoints officers, 95; biography, 133; orders parish assemblies to select officers, 76–77, 81, 83, 85, 97, 99; reconnaissance for Americans, 70; recruits Canadians, 82, 102; signal fires, 104

Gouin, Louis, 34, 50, 130; almost dismissed, 35; collects fines, 36; threatened by rebels, xxxvi, 49–50

Grant, William, 22, 129

Gravé de la Rive, Henri-François, 13, 128

Haldimand, Frederick, xlii, 126

Hazen, Moses, 133

Hubert, Jean-François, 10, 127

Intolerable Acts, xiv, xxx

Jefferson, Thomas, xix

Juchereau Duchesnay, Antoine: biography, 133; wheat confiscated, 96, 102–3, 105

King's wood, 7, 9, 127

Langlois, Pierre, 28, 130

Le Comte Dupré, Jean-Baptiste, 23, 129

Le Guerne, François, 17, 128

Lebrun de Duplessis, Jean-Baptiste: biography, 133; confiscates wheat for Americans, 96, 102–3, 105; suspected spy, 96

Lesperance (Canadian rebel), 12–15, 127

Liénard de Beaujeu de Villemonde, Louis, 70, 102–3, 110, 133–34; biography, 128; commands loyalist militia, 14, 84, 86, 93, 95–100, 104, 108, 111, 114–15, 132, 134; rebels oppose, 58, 68, 92, 133

Littlejohn, Captain, 32, 130

Livingston, James, xxxvi, 124

Mabane, Adam, 22, 126, 128

MacKinnon, Donald, 80, 133

Maclean, Allan, 30, 132–33; biography, 129; fines *habitants*, 36; recruits, 27

Mariauchau D'Esgly, Louis-Philippe, 20, 128

Mesplet, Fleury de, xiii–xiv, xvi

Montgolfier, Etienne, 41, 130

Montgomery, Richard, xiv, xxvi, xxxix, 49; appoints officer, 127; captures British ships, 54, 129, 131–32; death of, xxxvi; joins Arnold, 129, 131; leads Canadian invasion, xxxiii–xxxiv, 128, 130, 133; and paper money, xxxviii; and siege of Quebec, xxxv

Montreal, xiv, xvi, xxvii, xxxi, 28, 36; Allen attacks, 128, 131; American envoy to, xxxii; Americans occupy, xiv, xxxiii–xxxiv, xxxviii–xxxix; Carleton gathers militia at, 16, 36, 128; loyalist activities in, xl

Murray, James: appoints officers, 24–26, 34; appoints vicar general, 130; governor, xxx, 123

Old Subjects, xxxvi, xli–xlii; oppose Quebec Act, xxxi–xxxii

Michigan State University Press is committed to preserving ancient forests and natural resources. We have elected to print this title on Nature's Natural, which is 90% recycled (50% post-consumer waste) and processed chlorine free. As a result of our paper choice, Michigan State University Press has saved the following natural resources*:

6.96	Trees (40 feet in height)
2,030	Gallons of Water
1,189	Kilowatt-hours of Electricity
17.4	Pounds of Air Pollution

Both Michigan State University Press and our printer, Thompson-Shore, Inc., are members of the Green Press Initiative—a nonprofit program dedicated to supporting book publishers, authors, and suppliers in maximizing their use of fiber that is not sourced from ancient or endangered forests. For more information about the Green Press Initiative and the use of recycled paper in book publishing, please visit *www.greenpressinitiative.org.*

*Environmental benefits were calculated based on research provided by Conservatree and Californians Against Waste.